Of Broad Stripes and Bright Stars

Of Broad Stripes and Bright Stars

Gallantry over Bucharest

Jerry W. Whiting

Of Broad Stripes and Bright Stars
Copyright 2014 by Jerry Whiting
All rights reserved

First edition

Cover design by: Sherri Ortegren

ISBN 13: 978-0692270974

Library of Congress Control Number: 2014914166

Published by
Tarnaby
2576 Fox Circle
Walnut Creek, CA 94596

EAJWWhiting@aol.com

Except for brief quotes, no part of this book may be reproduced by any means without written permission of the author.

PRINTED IN THE UNITED STATES OF AMERICA

DEDICATION

I dedicate this book to the next generations, to those who haven't forgotten and who realize the importance of remembering and preserving our precious American history as it occurred, in a truthful and accurate manner.

Table of Contents

Acknowledgments		ix
Introduction		1
Prologue		5
Chapter 1	Target Bucharest	9
Chapter 2	Into the Cauldron	23
Chapter 3	The Hudson Owen Crew	33
Chapter 4	Flak Shak Attacked	39
Chapter 5	The Ivan Tyer Crew	57
Chapter 6	The John Crouchley Crew	65
Chapter 7	A Broader Picture	81
Epilogue		87
Appendix A	Bob Hickman V.A. Summary	95
Appendix B	Silver Star citation	97
Appendix C	Leasure letter	99
Photo Credits		101
References		103
Index		109

Acknowledgments

Bob Bobier
John Bybee and SPG
Paul Canin
Ovidiu Coca
Bill Cummings
Dick Doyle
Lee Dushkin
Agnes Hall
Bill Harrington
Bob Hickman
Ben Karoly
Dianne LaScotte
Sime Lisica
Richard Mattison
Dan Mortenson
Dick Olson
Leif Ortegren
Charlie Palmer
Jim Scheib
Roland Stumpf
Ann Whiting
John Wilson Jr

Harriet Butchko
Jonathan Caine
Vernon Christensen
Dan Crouchley
Phil Cummings
Henry Dahlberg
Linda Haley
Randy Hannum
Ray Heskes
Bob Johnson
Peter Kassak
Marvin Lindsay
Al Martin
Perry Monroe family
Matt Mortimer
Sandra Oprescu
Sherri Ortegren
Rabe Family
Stan Stanev
Wilson Shimer
Bill Williams
Arina Yuers

I want to especially acknowledge the assistance of Mark LaScotte and Sherri Ortegren. Mark is the true expert on the June 28, 1944 air battle over Rumania and Bulgaria and I couldn't have written the book without his assistance. He also provided the basic cover concept. Sherri Ortegren designed the cover and provided invaluable assistance with the overall look inside the book. Lee Dushkin and my wife, Ann, stepped in to rescue me during the editing phase.

Introduction

The "H" word has been redefined in modern society. Formerly it was reserved to describe those acts of courage which required extreme personal risk or danger, coupled with not quitting in the face of adversity. It was often used to describe actions that occurred in the military, but it was also used for civilians who acted in a manner that met the requirements for the definition. The possibility of future risk or danger was not enough for someone to fit the description of the "H" word; that person must have already acted in a certain manner while exposed to the risk or danger. So there had to be an element of risk or danger and courageous behavior while actually exposed to the risk.

Perhaps it's a reflection of our society that the "H" word, **Hero**, has changed and is now used almost daily and casually by the news media. It has gradually crept into our everyday vocabulary. For example, I recently watched a TV news story on a police academy graduation, describing the cadets as "future heroes". I've also heard it used to describe anyone who enlists in our military. I've heard it used in other ways, too. I cringed when I heard it used by the mother of an elementary school student who called the student a hero for getting a good grade on a report cord. Joining the military or becoming a police officer is honorable and certainly deserves our utmost respect, but in my book if falls short of meeting the definition of hero…getting a good grade in school doesn't even come close.

I would ask that you think of this word and an appropriate definition as you read about the men in this book. You may just find that many of them fit an earlier definition. Our military certainly thought so, bestowing them with appropriate awards. The term "gallantry in action" is used to describe the efforts of some of the men you'll read about in this book, the term used in their Silver Star citation. That's why I used the word "gallantry" in the subtitle of this book. All of them deserve to have their story told, and that's the reason I focused on several crews. Many medals were awarded that day, but medals only represent a few of the witnessed events and individuals.

For me, the research and writing of this book has been much different from previous efforts. It started many years ago when I was working on another book, writing about a copilot by the name of Matt Hall, who lost his life on a combat mission to Auschwitz, Poland. I learned more about his original crew, the crew of *Flak Shak*, and made a note to myself to learn more about them. I've done that. My research led me to a particular mission, the June 28, 1944 combat mission to Bucharest, Rumania and to other participants and an even broader story.[1]

I've personally met with a few of the men you'll read about, but not many, since most of those who survived that day have passed on. One of the men I've gotten to know is Bob Hickman. When I discussed with him the actions of his crew described in this book, I had a difficult time believing the story. I knew he was telling me what he believed to be true, and I didn't doubt his honesty and integrity the least bit, but what happened to him and his crew, and the way in which they responded, seemed nearly unbelievable. Had the element of time added to the story? Little did I know that when I reviewed reports and medical records from the time, and interviewed other eyewitnesses, I learned Bob was actually downplaying his role! That's so typical of these Vets. There is no shortage of bravery among the men whose stories I've told in this book.

One element that was different in the writing of this book is the important role of members of the next generation(s) who went to great efforts to locate and share with me documents from the time period when memories were fresh, of personal accounts from letters, diaries and journals, and of precious family history. In many cases these documents were more helpful than the official records, in part because they were more personal, and because they also described some of the events more specifically and accurately than the official documents. Many of the official chronicles and records, such as the Narrative Mission Report for that particular mission, are summary documents, a few pages written by one man to describe the incident, taken from oral debriefing interviews of 250 or 300 airmen. A diary or letter describes what one man saw. Both are important and helpful, but in different ways.

As always, I'm indebted to the Vets for trusting me to tell their story and I'm ever so appreciative to the next generations for keeping the memories alive by sharing these priceless elements of their family history. I hope you enjoy the book.

NOTES AND REFERENCES

[1] The other book was *Don't Let the Blue Star Turn Gold*.

Prologue

He couldn't explain it, but it was just one of those feelings. On June 27, 1944 after finishing dinner, 23 year-old Sgt. Eugene LaScotte checked the mission board for the next day and saw that he and 2nd Lt. John "Dud" Crouchley's crew were scheduled to fly. For some reason it just didn't feel right. He walked back to his tent, not knowing what to make of it.

It was a hot, humid night in southern Italy, even hotter and stickier than his home in St. Paul, Minnesota this time of year. LaScotte was the nose gunner on a B-24 bomber in the 828th Bomb Squadron of the 485th Bomb Group. He got ready to go to bed, knowing the next day would be a long one. He said nothing about his uneasiness to the other five gunners from his crew who lived in the same tent with him. They had flown a rough mission on the 26th, with lots of fighters and flak (anti-aircraft fire), to Vienna. Maybe this was at least part of the reason he was feeling this way.[1]

He stretched out on his army issue cot, but the uneasy feeling remained. He wasn't new to combat, having completed 19 missions with his crew, but he had never had this feeling before. He felt kind of sick, but didn't know if he was really ill or if it was just his nerves. It wasn't easy to fall asleep in this hot weather, with mosquitoes buzzing around his face and knowing he'd face combat the next day, but he finally dozed off.

He was awakened about 2:00AM for the mission. He quickly dressed and went with the others to the mess tent for breakfast. Like many of the airmen he didn't eat much on days he flew combat. After breakfast he went to the briefing, where he

Figure 1-Sgt. Eugene LaScotte

learned he was going to Bucharest, Rumania, not far from the Ploesti oil fields. He and his crew had already been to Ploesti and he didn't relish the thought of going anywhere in that country. He still felt uneasy and thought of going to sick call, but didn't want to get behind on his missions. Besides, his crew depended on him. After picking up his parachute and flying gear, a truck took him and his crew out to their assigned bomber.[2]

Across the field T/Sgt. James Scott, a radio operator/waist gunner from the 829th squadron, stood alongside the bomber checking out his flight gear. Today would be his 22nd combat mission flying with Lt. Ivan Tyer's crew. The copilot, 2nd Lt. Dick Jordan, was walking around the plane, checking the flight surfaces. Jordan approached Scott, looked around to make sure no one was near and said quietly "I have a bad feeling about this mission." Scott answered "Jordan, I've never felt this way before but I have the same feeling." Soon the crews entered their bombers. Less than five hours later, only one of these two men would be alive.[3]

Some would have years to reflect on their feelings about the mission that day. Others wouldn't be so fortunate.

Figure 2-S/Sgt. James Scott

Figure 3-2nd Lt. Dick Jordan

NOTES AND REFERENCES

[1] The 485th Bomb Group received the Distinguished Unit Citation for the June 26, 1944 mission to the Florisdorf Oil Refinery, Vienna, Austria. On this mission they penetrated intense, accurate, heavy caliber flak and were attacked by an estimated 35-40 German fighters. Only one bomber was lost.

[2] LaScotte expressed these feeling in an undated letter he wrote to his mother from a POW camp, but which was not received until after he returned home several months later.

[3] Scott referenced his premonition in his unpublished memoir.

Target Bucharest

There was no breeze to offer even remote relief from the stifling heat in the tent areas in this former wheat field in southern Italy. A mile from the airfield, the men of the 485th Bomb Group went about their business. Most of the airmen had already been down to look at the mission board. Those scheduled for a mission the next morning were getting ready to retire, hoping to get a decent night's rest on their army cots, although this would be difficult. The six enlisted men from each crew shared a tent, as did the four officers. Each of the four squadrons in the 485th Bomb Group had a separate tent area. A few of the men went to their respective enlisted men's club or officer's club, hoping to get their mind off flying the next day. Others wrote letters home or just went to bed.

The men scheduled to fly didn't know where they were going, only that they would be going into combat. They'd learn the target at the morning briefing. Some of the men thought of previous missions, to places like Wiener Neustadt, Munich, Vienna, and Ploesti, hoping Lady Luck would intervene and give them a milk run, an easy mission, for a change. They'd been on some really rough ones recently.

Living conditions were primitive, which didn't make things any easier. The group arrived just two months previously and set up their tents and had latrines built. Now, on the evening of June 27, 1944 the conditions were livable, but certainly not comfortable. Many of the men spent their free time improving the quality of their living conditions. Some extended their tents, made floors from local tufa block or scrap wood, or purchased woven matting from the locals for floor covering. Most had found some sort of a lamp or lantern to provide some light. Since there was no kerosene available, aviation gasoline was used as a fuel source, creating a few explosions as they were lit. Just two months ago the nights were cold, but now they were hot, making for difficult sleeping under any circumstances.

Insects were a huge problem in this open field. The ants were everywhere. There were also other tent mates including, crickets, flies, grasshoppers, and locusts. There was no escaping them. Field mice, too, invaded the tent areas.

There were several empty tents, a stark reminder that combat was serious business. Some of the occupied tents had empty cots, an even more personal reminder of the hazards of combat as this indicated that one or more men from the crew which shared that tent were wounded, prisoners or killed. Replacements were slowly coming in, but the group was still down in numbers. To complicate matters, the 485th lost 154 men when the Liberty Ship *S.S. Paul Hamilton* was sunk on April 20th. Most of these were ground personnel, but many of the crews that flew overseas gave up one airman to make room for key non-flying personnel. All of these flyers were lost in the sinking of the *Hamilton*.[1]

As darkness descended on the base, the sounds of life in the tent areas quieted. The occasional sound of a jeep could still be heard, but the voices diminished, and the sounds of crickets replaced them. In the distance, if one listened closely and there was a breeze, one could hear the sounds of a B-24 engine as the mechanics worked through the night to ready the planes for the next mission. The June 26th mission to Vienna was another rough one, with several planes returning with heavy battle damage and wounded aboard.[2] Planes were in short supply, so the mechanics worked feverishly to make the planes flyable for the mission the next day. There were no hangars and all repairs and maintenance were done outdoors. Across southern Italy, the same actions were occurring at other B-24 bases.[3]

At 2:00AM men with flashlights could be seen going from tent to tent, awakening the crews scheduled to fly. The men got up, some grumbling, and dressed. Although it was warm on the ground, it was bitter cold at 20,000 ft. or higher. Most of the men wore several clothing layers in the air, which could include pajamas, long underwear, pants and shirt, and a heated flying suit or fleece lined coat and pants. There were no wash facilities, so the men washed their faces in a water-filled helmet or pan before stumbling through the darkness to a squadron mess tent. The food was little better than the K rations they ate when they first arrived. Greasy pancakes and powdered eggs were often the fare. These didn't go well on a nervous stomach and many of the men just opted for the hot coffee. The cooks had little to work with, so they weren't to blame.

After breakfast the airmen went to their briefing. Today there were lots of groans when the curtain was pulled back and the target was revealed, the Titan Oil Storage tanks in Bucharest, Rumania. It was another major effort and the 485th Bomb Group would supply 39 aircraft. The three other groups in the 55th Bomb Wing would also be going to Bucharest. Two groups in the wing, the 464th and 465th, both based nearby at Pantanella, would lead the wing, breaking off at the I.P. (Initial Point) to bomb the Prahova refinery in Bucharest. The 485th was third in line. The 460th Bomb Group, based several miles away at Spinazzola, would follow the 485th and would also bomb the Titan Oil Storage tanks. The 485th would attack in two waves, trailing each other, each with three boxes of six or seven aircraft. Major Robert Smith, 485th Bomb Group operations officer, would lead the first wave and Captain Ralph Monroe, the 828th Squadron operations officer, would lead the second wave.

It would be one long formation going to Rumania, with P-38 fighter escorts to the target, P-51 escorts in the target area, and then another P-38 group providing protection on the way home. The bomb load would be ten 500 lb. bombs and their bombing altitude would be 23,800 feet. The scheduled target time was 10:00AM.

Following the 55th Bomb Wing to Bucharest would be the three bomb groups from the 49th Bomb Wing (451st, 461st and 484th).

Their target was the Chitila Marshaling Yard. Altogether, more than 150 B-24's were scheduled to bomb Bucharest. Meanwhile, the 304th Bomb Wing, consisting of the 454th, 455th, 456th and 459th Bomb Groups would form a parallel stream as they crossed the Adriatic Sea and then break off to the south to bomb the Karlova Airdrome in Bulgaria.

The call sign today for the 485th leader would be "Scanty 13". The other group leaders had similar call signs, which were changed for every mission. The code word for recalling the bombers was "Crime".

Intelligence showed that the flak guns in and around Bucharest were 75mm guns, as many as 126 batteries, reportedly manned by Rumanian personnel. The men could expect the flak to be intense, with probable low accuracy. The guns were not aided by radar. There was also a possibility that as many as 75 single-engine fighters and 15 twin-engine fighters could intercept the bomb group near the target.[4]

The missions to Rumania were all about oil and destroying the Axis oil producing capability. Ploesti was where the major refineries were in Rumania. The first Ploesti raid was in August 1942, a high-level raid from North Africa with just a few aircraft. The second raid was in August 1943, the famous low-level raid. Now, in mid-1944 there were regular, often costly bombing missions to Ploesti and surrounding areas where the oil was produced or stored, awaiting transportation to the German war effort. Most of the men flying this mission had already flown missions to Ploesti. The briefing officer told the men that any planes with seriously wounded aboard should land at Bari, on the east coast of Italy, where they had a fully-equipped hospital. Those with minor injuries could land at their home base.

The briefing officer explained the importance of the mission, stating that the two Bucharest facilities, Prahova and Titan, were putting out 250,000 tons of oil per year. Many of the men weren't too concerned or interested in the strategic importance of this (or any other) mission. Their main concern this morning was returning safely from this one. The briefing finished with a prayer from the chaplain, a comfort to some and a reminder to all that this was a deadly business.

The enlisted men, flight engineers, radio operators, armorer/gunners and career gunners[5] were the first to board the trucks to take the mile ride to the flight line after picking up their flight gear. The trucks dropped a few men off at each plane, then proceeded to another plane where they did the same, before going back to pick up more men. The flight engineers usually met with the crew chief assigned to each plane to see if there were any issues the crew needed to be aware of regarding the airplane's condition. The radio operator checked his equipment in the plane and the armorer/gunner checked the guns. The other gunners checked their equipment, their guns, or just waited for the officers to arrive.

A few minutes later the trucks returned, stopping near each plane, dropping off the officers. Over at *Flak Shak*, 2nd Lt. Volney "Bud" Wiggins, the pilot, walked around the plane, checking the control surfaces[6]. He was accompanied by 2nd Lt. Matt Hall, the copilot. Wiggins was one of the more experienced pilots in the group, having been a flight instructor at Boise, Idaho before being assigned to the 485th Bomb Group, 831st Squadron, when it was formed in Fairmont, Nebraska in late 1943.

Wiggins' talents were well-known in the squadron, especially after an earlier mission. On this mission the plane suffered severe flak damage. The ball turret was jammed in the down position and couldn't be repaired in the air. The ball gunner was stuck inside the turret, unable to rotate the turret to a position where he could climb into the aircraft. In a B-24 the ball turret retracted into the body of the aircraft. Not only couldn't the turret be retracted, but the ball gunner, Cpl. Hartupee, was stuck inside the turret. This was an extremely dangerous situation. If the landing gear collapsed from battle damage or a rough landing, the ball gunner would be crushed beneath the plane. When they arrived back at the base, the control tower had Wiggins land last. Since the other crews had already landed and were aware of the situation, many watched as Wiggins lined up on the field. He made a perfect landing. The happiest guy on the crew was Hartupee, who faced certain death if the landing had been anything less than perfect.[7]

Figure 4-Front Row, Left to Right: 2nd Lt. Matt Hall, copilot; 2nd Lt. John Dempsey, bombardier; 2nd Lt. Volney Wiggins, pilot, and 2nd Lt. Ken Leasure, navigator. Back Row, Left to right: T/Sgt. Wilson Shimer, waist gunner/flight engineer; M/Sgt. Stacy Hayes, crew chief; S/Sgt. Virgil Anderson, top turret/flight engineer; S/Sgt. Martin Caine, radio operator/waist gunner; S/Sgt. Francis Brittain, nose gunner, and Cpl. Edward Hartupee, ball gunner.

Both Wiggins and Hall were married. The 20 year-old Hall, a Georgia native, was hoping to finish his missions and return home to his wife, Jean, before his 21st birthday in November. Hall had originally checked out as a 1st pilot in Salt Lake City, but there was an excess of 1st pilots and Hall was sent back into the pool, to emerge as a copilot assigned to the 485th. Consequently, Hall had more training and experience than many other copilots in the 485th. Together, they made a great team. Most of the crew had flown 24 or 25 missions since their arrival in Italy. The crew chief, M/Sgt. Stacy Hayes, met briefly with the pilots to provide an update on the plane's condition.[8]

2nd Lt. Ken Leasure, the navigator, lived in Pennsylvania before the war. He was more reserved, serious-minded and analytical than the others. He kept to himself quite a bit, but was an excellent navigator and was well-respected by the entire crew. When the crew originally flew overseas, Leasure's ETA at the airfield where they landed was less than 30 seconds different than their actual arrival time, no small feat when crossing the Atlantic Ocean. On that day he made a name for himself on the crew. Leasure carried his map case and placed it in the navigator's compartment in the nose of the aircraft.

2nd Lt. John Dempsey, the bombardier, was more outgoing than Leasure. Dempsey was friendly and talkative. He was very likable and quick to greet the other crew members waiting. At his station in the front of the plane he checked the intervolometer settings for the bombs, the mechanism that measured the time sequence between the release of each bomb in the bomb load.

Pvt. Bob Hickman, the 19 year-old tail gunner, had already checked out his guns before the officers arrived. Like the others on this crew, he threw the bag containing his gear into the plane through the rear hatch. The Ohio native was the newest and youngest man on the crew. He had been trained as an armorer/gunner in the U.S. before he ran afoul of a lieutenant at a base in New Mexico, was demoted and sent overseas in December 1943. After his arrival in January he was assigned to help build the base at Venosa. One of his primary assignments was laying down the PSP (metal planking) that formed the runway. When the Hamilton was sunk in April, the 485th was short of gunners. Hickman immediately volunteered and was assigned Wiggins' crew. On earlier missions he had quickly proven himself a valuable asset and was a welcome member of the crew.[9]

Figure 5-Robert Hickman

When Hickman first entered the plane to check out the guns in his turret, he saw Cpl. Edward "Lyle" Hartupee inside the waist section of the plane. Hartupee liked to drink a bit and he had a routine of plugging his oxygen mask into one of the oxygen stations in the plane, turning it to 100% and giving himself a dose of oxygen to clear his head and get rid of the lingering effects of the alcohol from the previous night. Hartupee had enlisted in the Army in 1940. The 26 year-old gunner was originally assigned to a B-26 group in the U.S. before being transferred to the 485th and assigned to the ball turret.

S/Sgt. Virgil Anderson, the 24 year-old top turret gunner and flight engineer from Benson, Minnesota, was another friendly, likable guy. There were two flight engineers on the crew, Anderson and T/Sgt. Wilson Shimer. Wilson was a Pennsylvania native who had joined the Army in 1939, having graduated from high school the year before. Jobs were still scarce due to the Depression and Shimer thought the military might be a good fit. He had become a flight engineer and was an instructor at Boise, checking out new flight engineers. He had flown frequently with Wiggins there and they developed a mutual respect for one another. When Wiggins was assigned to the 485 Bomb Group, which was being formed in Fairmont, Nebraska, Wiggins asked him to be his flight engineer. Both Shimer and Anderson had spoken to Hayes before the pilots arrived, confirming the plane was in good condition and ready for the mission.[10]

S/Sgt. Brittain was the nose gunner. He was single, good-looking and from Georgia. He was a real ladies man.

S/Sgt. Martin Caine was the radio operator and manned the left waist gun. Caine had earned a reputation as a scrounger. He was from New York, friendly to everyone and liked to talk. He was instrumental in making improvements to their tent because he seemed to be able to acquire things that others couldn't. He had also been spearheading the creation of the 831st Squadron club/bar for the enlisted men at the base.

Figure 6-T/Sgt. Wilson Shimer; Cpl. Edward Hartupee; S/Sgt. Martin Caine, and S/Sgt. Virgil Anderson. (Crew mascots "Butch" and "Wutch" are being held by the men.)

The name of the aircraft would have significant meaning by the end of the day. "Flak" was the term for anti-aircraft fire. A "Shak" was slang often used by bombardiers meaning a direct hit. The plane has a blue "W" painted on the side of the plane, behind the waist window and the letter was the radio call sign for the plane. In the 831st Sqdn the letter used was often the first letter of the pilot's last name.

Other crews were checking out their planes. 2nd Lt. Robert Sloan, another 831st pilot, had recently acquired his own crew. He replaced another pilot who had become the copilot with another crew. Sloan had originally been assigned to the group as a copilot, but was selected as a 1st pilot because of his demonstrated abilities.

Figure 7-Lt. Robert Sloan

Across the field, Lt. Ivan Tyer's 829th Sqdn crew was preparing for the mission. Radio operator T/Sgt. Scott couldn't shake the uneasiness he felt as he checked out the radio. The earlier conversation with his copilot, 2nd Lt. Jordan, compounded this feeling. Their assigned plane, *Tyer's Flyers*, was being repaired and for the first time they were flying in a different plane. There was still a shortage of aircraft in the group, so they were flying *Nudist Kay*, a B-24 assigned to the 830th Sqdn. This aircraft had been severely damaged on the June 26th mission and the mechanics raced to get it ready for the mission. This didn't make Scott feel any better. He'd much prefer to be in his own plane. They were Tail-End Charlie again and would be flying as the last plane in their box. It seemed to Scott that they had flown this position much more than they deserved. Being the last plane made them more vulnerable to fighter attacks. The ball gunner, S/Sgt. Horace O'Connor, somehow incurred the wrath of the squadron commander, Captain Boney and was now a private. This didn't help morale much. O'Connor was a good man and a good gunner.[11]

2nd Lt. Crouchley's 828th Sqdn crew was ready for the mission. Their aircraft, *Miss Yankee Rebel*, was being repaired, having run off the end of the runway with another crew, so they also were flying a different plane today. LaScotte, the nose gunner, still had the feelings of the previous night, but couldn't do much about it. He cleaned the Plexiglas windows on his nose turret as he waited. The crew's regular navigator, Allen Meister, was becoming a lead navigator and today 2nd Lt. Bill Hollowell was taking his place. The regular bombardier, 2nd Lt. Forrest Leveille, was still at rest camp and was being replaced by 2nd Lt. John Wilson from another crew. Both Meister and Wilson were originals in the group and had flown many of the group's early missions. LaScotte noted that Wilson seemed very serious. That was a good thing, because this combat was a serious business.

Crouchley had just returned from rest camp the previous day. The flight surgeon decided he and Leveille needed a rest after an earlier rough mission where Leveille received some minor flak wounds in the foot and temple. They were due to return the previous day after some much needed rest, but the plane that came to pick them up blew a tire and damaged a wheel. It was a small landing strip and the B-24 would not be repaired until the next day. Leveille was happy to get another day of relaxation, while Crouchley was anxious to get back to base. His wife was expecting a baby any day and he was hoping to get some good news. Another plane brought some more men to camp and Crouchley managed to hitch a ride back to base, in time for him and the rest of the crew to be put on the mission board for the next day.[12]

Figure 8-Miss Yankee Rebel with some of her crew

Wilson had been looking forward to a day off, when he was awakened and told he'd be flying that day with another crew. He wasn't real happy about it and didn't know the crew, but was impressed with their professionalism when he met them on the field.[13]

2nd Lt. Hudson Owen and his crew were also readying their plane, *My Brother and I*. The story behind the naming of the plane was interesting. Lt. Owen's brother was a B-26 pilot stationed in Sardinia. Shortly after Owen arrived in Italy he learned his brother had been killed. The 828th Sqdn crew named their plane in honor of the brother's loss. This crew had already suffered its share of losses. On the June 26th mission to Vienna, both the tail gunner, S/Sgt. Herman Maurer, and the top turret gunner, S/Sgt. George Mack III went down while flying with another crew. The crew was still reeling from these recent losses, but this was war and two other gunners were assigned to fly with them on this mission.[14]

Shortly after 5:00AM the men began crawling into the big bombers and several minutes later the order came to start the engines. There were loud popping noises, engines backfiring, followed by the

Figure 9-Front Row, Left to Right: 2nd Lt. Fales Halcomb, navigator; 2nd Lt. Jerry Durden, bombardier; 2nd Lt. Hudson Owen, pilot and 2nd Lt. William Roberts, copilot. Back Row, Left to Right: Sgt. Herman Maurer, tail gunner; Sgt. George Mack, top turret gunner; Sgt. Alfred Aborjaily, radio operator/waist gunner; Sgt. Perry Monroe, ball gunner; Sgt. Ken Ponte, nose gunner and Sgt. Joe Coker, waist gunner.

roar of the engines as they came to life, smoke pouring from their exhausts and then finally evening out. The sound of 156 engines thundered across the plain. One by one the planes left their hardstands, brakes squealing, as they taxied to the end of the field. When the green flare was shot from the control tower the planes began taking off, in 30-second intervals.

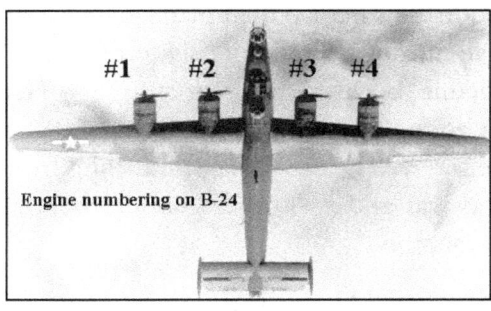

Figure 10-Top view of B-24 aircraft

NOTES AND REFERENCES

[1] The S.S. Paul Hamilton, a liberty ship, was sunk off the coast of Algiers in an aerial attack. All aboard were killed and it is reputed to be the largest human loss on a liberty ship during WWII.

[2] The 485th Bomb Group later received the Distinguished Unit Citation for their accomplishments on this mission.

[3] None of the six B-17 bomb groups in Italy were scheduled for a mission on June 28, 1944

[4] The source of the intelligence information provided at briefing was the 55th Bomb Wing Operations Order #108

[5] Gunners with no additional training were called career gunners

[6] The ranks of the men on this crew are as of June 26th, two days before the mission. Several of the crew received promotions shortly after the mission.

[7] This landing was witnessed by 831st Sqdn ball gunner Ray Heskes. He related it to the author in a 2005 phone conversation and also summarized it in an email letter to Linda Haley, dated December 22, 2004.

[8] The information about Hall's previous status as a 1st pilot was revealed in an 11/15/43 letter home.

[9] Background info on Hickman from telephone interviews with him on 1/19/11 and 6/20/14.

[10] Background info on Shimer from telephone interview by author on 3/2/11. Both Shimer and Hickman provided the background details on the other crew members.

[11] These details are from Scott's self-published memoir.

[12] This rest camp was likely Villagio Mancuso, a camp set up for officers. The information about Crouchey and Leveille going to camp was revealed in contact the LaScotte family had with Leveille in August 2000.

[13] This information was revealed in an email to the author from John Wilson Jr. on July 7, 2014 from a conversation Wilson had with his father before his death.

[14] The loss of these men was referenced in the diary of ball gunner Perry Monroe.

Into the Cauldron

B-24's were taking off from bases across southern Italy. The 39 planes from the 485th began taking off at 5:48AM. They formed into 3-plane elements, then the two elements joined to become boxes, circling their assigned area near Altamura. Once they were assembled in boxes, they assembled into two separate waves, three boxes in each wave. This all took time, nearly an hour, but by 6:43AM they had completed their assembly.

Once assembled, the lead plane led them to Spinazzola, where they made their rendezvous with the other groups from their wing at 7:11AM. They fell into a loose formation behind the 464th Bomb Group. Ahead of the 464th, leading the mission, was the 465th Bomb Group. This assembly took more time. The groups continued to climb, circling the area, and were joined by the 460th Bomb Group, which fell into its assigned position behind the 485th, at 8:00AM. Once assembled into their wing formation, they headed east across the Adriatic Sea.

As the squadrons formed up, Eugene LaScotte was in the front of his plane. It would still be quite a while before Lt. Crouchley, the pilot, gave the order for the gunners to get in their turrets and test their guns, so he was just sitting in the nose of the plane, looking out a side window. He remembered that June 28th was his mother's birthday. He thought of her and the others at home and wondered what she had planned for the day back in St. Paul. There wasn't much for him to do so he switched the control on his intercom connection to listen to Armed Forces Radio for a few minutes. The station was in Bari and provided a real morale boost to the airmen. Normally his crew would listen to the station while returning home from a mission, after they left enemy territory when it was safe. While he was listening on this channel he couldn't hear communications on the intercom, so he didn't want to listen for too long.

When LaScotte switched channels he recognized his favorite D.J. This guy always made him laugh. Today the announcer was mad, having been called a "drugstore cowboy", by someone, all in fun, of course. The announcer said something like "Come on down to the studio and I'll show you who's a drugstore cowboy." LaScotte got a chuckle out of that and made a mental note to stop in and meet the announcer some time if he made it back from this mission. There, it happened again. He'd never said "if" before, so why did he have this thought today? He switched back to the intercom and tried to get his mind on something else.[1]

James Scott was still feeling uneasy about this mission as he stood looking out the waist window. The other gunners on Tyer's crew were waiting for the pilot to tell them to test fire their guns. He hadn't checked the .50 caliber machinegun before take-off because he had been talking to Lt. Jordan, so he looked the gun over. He couldn't believe his eyes when he saw the firing pin bolt was missing from the gun. Without it the gun was useless. If they'd been in their own plane, this wouldn't have happened. Their ground crew was really efficient and careful. He wondered if the plane was jinxed. He started looking around for the bolt and found it lying on the floor. Someone must have cleaned the gun and forgot to replace the bolt. It was a stupid mistake and one that could easily cost the crew their lives. Shortly after he reassembled the gun the pilot gave the order to test their guns and he fired a few rounds. The gun worked fine, but he still didn't feel good about this one.[2]

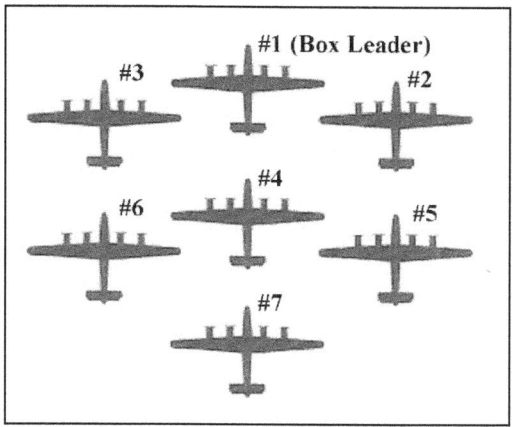

Figure 11-Typical 7-plane box

There were now two columns of B-24's heading east across the Adriatic Sea. The column on the right was the 304th Bomb Wing, the group totaling more than 100 bombers. This group would later break off and turn south to bomb the Karlova airdrome in Bulgaria. On the left, the longer column contained the 229 planes from the 55th and 49th Bomb wings, both assigned to targets in the Bucharest Area.

Shortly after they were over water they were joined by their escorts, three squadrons of P-38 fighters from the 1st Fighter group. The fighters flew several thousand feet higher than the bombers and were weaving between the two bomber columns. To the bomber crews looking up at them it was a comforting sight.

Shortly after 9:00AM the 304th Wing made a sweeping turn to the right, crossing the Danube River, now headed for their target in Bulgaria. One squadron of fighters followed this formation, while the other two squadrons from the 1st Fighter Group continued their weaving patterns over the B-24's that were going to Bucharest. The scheduled target time was 10:00AM and the groups from the 55th Bomb Wing were already several minutes ahead of schedule. As long as they had their escorts with them, it wasn't a problem and the P-38's were about 5,000 feet above the bombers now, so they had a good view of everything below them. Up until this point they hadn't seen any German fighters, at least not any close enough to the bombers to be considered a threat. The fighters were instructed not to leave the bombers to pursue the German fighters, unless the bombers were in danger of imminent attack.

The 485th held its position third in line as the formation entered Rumania, approaching 24,000 feet in altitude. At 9:45AM they were approaching the I.P. or Initial Point, where the group would turn onto the bomb run, when several of the airmen look up to see the P-38's leaving them. The P-51's providing the target cover weren't in view, but they must be up there.[3]

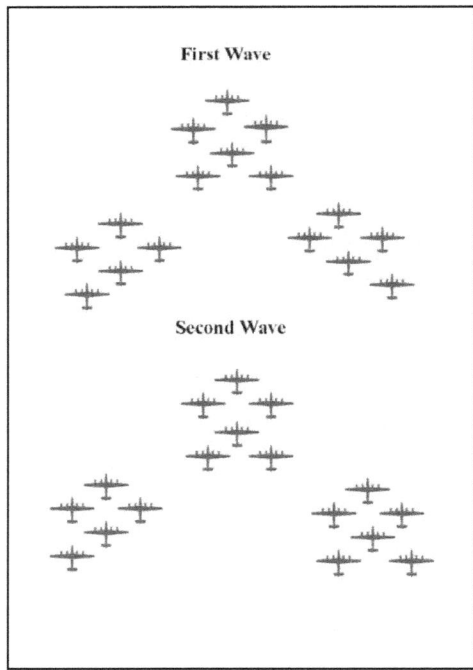

Figure 12-485th Attack formation over Bucharest

As soon as the bombers began their 4-minute bomb run, flak began bursting around them. At first it wasn't too close, but there was a lot of it. The Germans went to great efforts to protect their oil. The lead bombardier found the primary target obscured ahead of him at the beginning of the bomb run. A quick decision was made to bomb a secondary target, a factory in Bucharest and the first wave dropped their bombs 30 seconds later.[4]

Just before the first wave dropped their bombs, a group of ME-109's came out of the sun in a diving attack on the back of the first wave, damaging several bombers in both waves with cannon and machinegun fire as they passed between the waves. The lead bombardier in the second wave spotted the primary target, the Titan Oil Refinery, through the clouds and the second wave toggled their bombs on the refinery, scoring several hits. The German fighters were on them now. They seemed to be everywhere, aggressive attacks by swarms of ME-109's and FW 190's. They came from the front, the back and from the sides, from both above and below the formations. The gunners had their hands full, with the Germans coming in from two to six abreast and also attacking with two to four inline.

After several of the bombers were hit and straggled behind, Major Smith broke radio silence at 10AM, using his call sign of "Scanty 13" to request fighter support from "Exceed", the call sign for the P-51's of the 31st Fighter Group, their assigned escorts. There was no answer and the P-51's were nowhere to be seen. The fighter attacks continued for another 20 minutes. Most of the attacks were from ME-109's, although a variety of German aircraft were spotted in the target area, including ME-110's, a JU-88 and even a few JU-87 Stuka dive bombers, which did not attack.

At 10AM the 40 fighters from the 31st Fighter Group arrived in the target area, too late and too far away to be of any help to the 485th. Since the 485th was 10 minutes early over the target, they were now more than 25 miles ahead of the rendezvous point and the closest fighters. Even if the P-51's had heard the call, they couldn't have been of any help. The bombers were on their own.[5]

In reality, the 31st Fighter Group was assigned to rendezvous with the 55th Bomb Wing at 9:45AM, to provide top cover in the target area. They were three minutes late, arriving at the rendezvous point at 9:48AM, still several miles from the target, and many miles behind the 485th, which was already on the bomb run by that time.[6]

The P-38's of the 1st Fighter Group later reported they left the bomb groups where the P-51's awaited them. Could they possibly have mistaken the swarm of ME-109's waiting ahead for P-51's? Or had they seen some P-51's from the 325th Fighter Group which may have been in the same general area, since the 325th was assigned to a fighter sweep over the greater Bucharest area? Whatever the answer, it spelled big trouble for the 485th.[7]

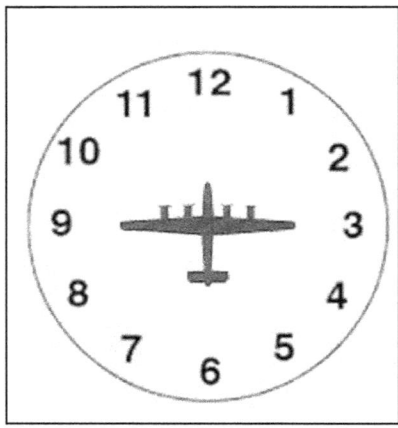

Figure 13-Clock positions as they relate to fighter attacks

It was estimated that 45 to 50 German fighters were seen in the target area with between 32 and 35 of them focusing their attacks on the 485th. The gunners who returned to base that day would later claim they shot down 12 ME-109's, probably destroyed 15 more and damaged an FW190.[8]

Shortly after the second wave dropped their bombs on the Titan Oil Refinery, German fighters attacked the low box (left side) of the formation. It was a frontal attack by six ME 109's. Lt. Sloan's plane was their target, flying on the left wing of the wave leader, in the #3 position. Three of the fighters attacked from 11 o'clock high, one after another, while three others followed, attacking from the 1 o'clock high position. They were diving attacks.⁹

Fig. 14- Captain Hanson

Captain John Hanson and his crew witnessed most of what happened to Lt. Sloan and his crew. He described it later.

*Lt. Sloan was flying #3 position on Captain Hogan's wing on the bomb run. Shortly after the completion of the bomb run six fighters attacked the lower box, a group of three from about 11 o'clock high, followed by another three from about 12-1 o'clock. The second plane of the second three fighters was shot down by S/Sgt Hufstader. The third fighter was assumed to have hit the #3 engine of Sloan's ship as the cowling was seen to fly off. At about the same time the #1 propeller was seen to feather and Lt. Sloan's ship fell back and out of formation, falling from view behind the left wing of my ship. Over the interphone my gunners kept me informed of Lt. Sloan. He was attacked by six fighters, then his landing gear was seen to come down with the ship still under control. The fighters followed, attacking and set the ship afire. The ship started down followed by fighters still attacking. Shortly before the ship hit the ground and burst into flames, two chutes appeared-the last about the same time as the ship hit. It crumpled on the ground almost immediately.*¹⁰

Lt. Bill Harrington was the bombardier on Captain Hanson's plane. He had just dropped his bombs when nine ME-109's tore through the formation, three of them in a frontal attack. After the attack he looked out from his position in the nose, watching Lt. Sloan's plane.

> *All this time I was watching Sloan. He had perfect control of his ship with its landing gear down. He did this because he was led to believe if the Jerry pilot saw you were finished, he would cease firing. He (Sloan) held the ship down to about 5000' when two ME 109's attacked from 8:30. When they peeled off, he (Sloan) went into a spin. Two chutes opened not more than 500' from the ground. The other eight men were in the ship when she spun into the ground and burst into flames.*[11]

None of the men from this crew survived, despite the parachutes seen coming out at low altitude. Two other planes were seen going down near the target area. A few minutes after the last German fighter left, the P-38's from the 82nd Fighter Group arrived to escort the bombers home. The P-38's actually arrived several minutes early, but were still too late to fend off any of the fighter attacks.[12]

Figure 15-Lt. Harrington

Several of the planes had wounded aboard and were heavily damaged. Of the planes from the 485th that made it back to Italy, 29 landed at Venosa and four landed at other friendly fields. The men in each of the planes had a story to tell that day, if they lived to tell it.[13]

NOTES AND REFERENCES

[1] LaScotte provided this information in a 7/28/98 interview with Dianne LaScotte. He had told this story many times over the years, according to other family members.

² Scott discussed this in his unpublished private account of the 6/28/44 mission.

³ Narrative Mission Report 1051 from the 1st Fighter group states, regarding the two squadrons covering the 55th Wing, "left the bombers at the appointed place, Cochinesti, where the P-51's awaited them, at 0945/0950 hours, at 24,000', to return to base.

⁴ The 485th BG information regarding times, targets, enemy fighter attacks, is from the 485th BG Narrative Mission Report for 6/28/44.

⁵ The 1st Fighter Group Narrative Mission Report #1051 reported moderate jamming of radio frequencies, so it's possible the jamming interfered with the call for help. The 52nd Fighter Group, which was providing cover for the 49th Bomb Wing, reported jamming of radio frequency B in the target area in Narrative Mission Report #33.

⁶ From 31st Fighter Group Narrative Mission Report #571.

⁷ From 1st Fighter Group Narrative Mission Report #1051.

⁸ German records recovered after the war didn't show nearly as many losses that day and they attributed most of their losses to American fighters.

⁹ The source of the details regarding what happened to Sloan's crew are five witness statements from MACR (Missing Air Crew Report) 6411, from men in various planes. The statements differ slightly, in minor detail, but are generally in agreement regarding the circumstances.

¹⁰ From Captain Hanson's statement in MACR 6411.

¹¹ From Bill Harrington's diary entry for 6/28/44.

¹² Although a total of three bombers were observed going down in the confusion of battle, only two B-24's were actually lost in the target area, Lt. Sloan's plane and Lt. Tyer's plane.

¹³ There were also some planes that returned early with mechanical problems.

The Hudson Owen Crew

Just before bombs away, seemingly out of nowhere, ME-109's and Me-110's shot through the formation, scoring several hits on *My Brother and I*. Simultaneously, the B-24 was damaged by a flak burst. S/Sgt. Ken Ponte, the nose gunner, spotted a ME-109 coming up from ten o'clock low and fired a burst at him. He saw pieces fall from the fighter and it dove away to the right, out of his view. The other gunners were also busy, shooting at the fighters as five of them made repeated passes on their box. S/Sgt. Perry Monroe claimed a Messerschmitt from his position in the ball turret and saw the plane explode as it passed beneath him. The attacks kept coming and the bomber struggled to maintain its position in the second wave.[1]

2nd Lt. Hudson Owen, the pilot, was badly wounded in the leg in an earlier attack. The copilot, 2nd Lt. Bill Roberts, was busy at the controls, trying to keep the plane in formation. Two of the engines were out, the hydraulic system was hit and the oxygen was knocked out at various stations. Several fuel cells were ruptured and one vertical stabilizer had severe damage. The plane gradually fell back from the formation, losing altitude, despite the pilots' efforts to stay with their group. The fighters were gone, but the plane was in bad shape.[2]

Ponte heard a banging on the nose turret door behind him. The bombardier, 2nd Lt. Jerry Durden and the navigator, 2nd Lt. Fales Halcomb were both banging on the door. They told him the pilot had rung the bailout bell, the signal to prepare to bail out. Ponte couldn't hear the bell in his turret, so he depended on others to keep him apprised, since communications were shot out. They helped him out of his turret and one of them handed him his parachute. He quickly snapped it onto to the two rings of the harness he was wearing.[3]

Figure 16-Front Row, Left to Right: Joe Coker, William Roberts, Hudson Owen, Jerry Durden, and Perry Monroe. Back Row, Left to Right: Alfred Aborjaily, George Mack, Ken Ponte, Herman Maurer, and Fales Halcomb.

Since communications had been shot out in the nose, the three men crouched by the nose wheel doors, waiting for the bell to ring again, the signal to jump. They hovered there for several minutes, but the bell didn't ring again. Durden finally decided to crawl back to the flight deck to see what was happening. He returned several minutes later, telling them what had happened.

Owen's leg wound was severe and he was in bad shape. 2nd Lt Bill Roberts had taken over the controls. Roberts had his hands full with the damaged plane, but didn't want anyone to bail out just yet. He was trying to nurse the plane back to Italy. By this time they were out of sight of the bomber formation, lagging far behind and approaching the eastern Adriatic coast.

Several minutes later, Ponte removed his parachute and made his way to the flight deck to see if he could be of assistance. As he climbed onto the flight deck he saw the left bomb bay door had been torn away and was flapping in the wind. He saw Owen on the flight deck, obviously in great pain, but conscious. The flight engineer was working feverishly, transferring fuel from the damaged cells, trying to get fuel to the two engines still running.

The engineer asked Ponte to let the men in the back of the plane know that they should prepare for ditching. The navigator had just reported that they didn't have enough fuel to make it and would have to ditch in the Adriatic Sea. Ponte slowly made his way on the catwalk through the bomb bay, seeing the holes in the plane from the fighter attacks. He told the men in the back of the plane to prepare for ditching and then helped them throw everything that was loose out of the bomber, hoping to lighten the load and get rid of any objects that could fly around, injuring the men if they ditched. Guns, ammo and anything not bolted down was thrown out the waist windows. When Ponte was satisfied that they'd accomplished this task, he made his way back through the plane and climbed onto the flight deck. As he passed through the bomb bay he noted that fluid was leaking everywhere, a clear sign that the hydraulics had been shot out. He told the engineer about the leaks, but the engineer was already aware of this. Ponte reported that the waist was ready for ditching, watching the engineer manipulate different valves, trying to get fuel to the two engines still running.

Figure 17-Ken Ponte

A few minutes later, as they were crossing the Adriatic, the navigator reported there was a possibility they might make it to the coast of Italy. Since the engineer was busy, Ponte said he'd put the U-lock on the nose wheel, a procedure done just before landing, and made his way to the nose. This wasn't a regular assignment for Ponte, but he had done it before and knew how to do it.

The engineer had to hand crank the main gear down, since the hydraulics were out. S/Sgt. Alfred Aborjaily, the radio operator put out a MAYDAY call as they approached land. They were trying to make it to the field at Bari, right on the coast. The flaps were inoperable due to the battle damage, so they were coming in fast, way too fast. Ponte waited for the nose wheel to drop after the main gear was down, then reached through the open doors and put the U-shaped lock on the nose gear.

His intent now was to get crawl back to the flight deck as quickly as possible, to his normal landing position. He glanced through the open nose wheel door and saw they were just a few feet above land. With no time to move back in the plane, he quickly put himself into a tucked position and faced the rear of the plane. He felt and heard the main gear touch down and that was the last thing he remembered.

It must have been several minutes later when Ponte regained consciousness, looked about and saw mangled pieces of metal all around him. He faded in and out of consciousness. He later recalled checking his arms and legs and realizing the right side of his body was trapped in the wreckage.

Ponte heard voices outside the wreckage and a voice was calling his name. He answered the voice and soon could hear the sounds of tearing metal as his rescuers cut through the metal skin of the plane alongside him. A few minutes later he heard a voice and was passed a canteen. He took a drink. The man identified himself as a doctor and said they were going to get him out. Soon he felt hands tugging at him, pulling him from the wreckage, placing him on a stretcher, and loading him into an ambulance. He saw a plasma bottle hooked to his arm and he was whisked away to the hospital at Bari.

In addition to the serious injuries to Owen and Ponte, Aborjaily, the radio operator suffered a shoulder injury and S/Sgt. Joe Coker split his head open in the crash. Monroe fractured a vertebrae. All survived their injuries.[4] Ponte would be sent back to the U.S. and spend 19 months in hospitals.

Figure 18- *My Brother and I* after landing at Bari

Figure 19- Perry Monroe being carried from the plane

Figure 20-Nose wreckage where Ken Ponte was trapped

Figure 21-Perry Monroe later receiving medals

NOTES AND REFERENCES

[1] Details are from Perry Monroe diary entry for 6/28/44.
[2] Ibid
[3] Details relating to Ken Ponte's activities are from a story he wrote about the mission, featured in ***This Is How it Was***.
[4] Both Fales Halcomb and Jerry Durden were later killed on the 7/20/44 mission to Friedrichschafen, Germany, when they were shot down by fighters while flying with another crew.

Flak Shak Attacked

Flak Shak was hit hard by flak on the bomb run. At the same time eight German ME-109's dove through the formation from 10 o'clock high, guns blazing, blowing holes in the left wing and damaging the #4 engine. Anderson was firing from the top turret. The German leader blew up as he passed beneath the bomber. Shimer fired a short burst at them from the right waist gun, but they were gone in a split second. Dempsey, at his bombsight, was hit by shellfire in his leg, nearly blowing the leg off. Despite the serious injury, he remained at the bombsight, toggling his bombs. Wiggins turned the big bomber to the right, leading his box in a diving turn away from the target.[1]

As Wiggins led his box in the rally off the target, fighters attacked again from in front and above. On this pass they knocked out the turbo on #1 engine and copilot Hall was hit several times with shrapnel from exploding cannon shells, knocking the headphones from his head, severing all radio communications throughout the plane and cutting off the oxygen supply to the positions in

Figure 22- 2nd Lt. Matt Hall

the nose. Anderson's top turret was hit by bullets, knocking some of the Plexiglas off, with a shell fragment lodging in the receiver of the machineguns directly in front of his face.

Flak Shak fell out of the lead position while losing power, and slipped beneath and to the right of the formation. Wiggins struggled at the controls, trying to stay with the group.

Hall had been peppered with shrapnel in his right arm and was bleeding from the injuries. Despite his condition, at Wiggins' direction, he climbed out of his seat, grabbed the portable oxygen bottles and made his way to the nose of the bomber. Nose gunner Brittain had been firing at the Messerschmitts in the first two attacks, and sent at least one of them away smoking. As Hall crawled into the nose compartment, he saw navigator Leasure, bleeding from minor shrapnel wounds of his own, trying to stop the flow of blood in Dempsey's leg and could see Brittain still in his turret, ready for the next attack. Leasure had already given Dempsey a shot of morphine to ease the pain. Hall gave the portable bottles to Leasure and crawled as quickly as possible back along the narrow passage to the entrance to the bomb bay, climbed onto the flight deck, taking the right hand seat alongside Wiggins.

Figure 23- Lt. Volney Wiggins

The bomber fell farther and farther behind the group and was now starting a dive. Wiggins and Hall both fought the damaged controls to bring the bomber out of the dive that was getting steeper. Both used all their strength, pulling back on the yokes and leveling out of the dive after losing several thousand feet of altitude. Leasure, having stopped most of the bleeding on Dempsey's leg, now made his way to the flight deck to assist the pilots. The hydraulic and electrical systems had suffered major damage. The radio system was completely knocked out.

Flak Shak Attacked

The bomber was now in big trouble. The fighters had accomplished their task, separating *Flak Shak* from the herd, so to speak. They were without the protection of the other bombers in the formation, just sitting ducks. Leasure discussed Dempsey's wounds with Wiggins, along with the condition of the bomber. Both knew they were in bad shape and Leasure gave Wiggins a general heading to reach the Yugoslavian coast. That was the best he could do.

The ME-109's now switched their attacks to the rear, having crippled the bomber and knocking it out of the formation. Hickman in the tail turret was ready for them as they came in from behind and above. Six or seven of them came diving in. Hickman fired short bursts, but wasn't sure he hit any of them. Hartupee opened up on them from the ball turret as they passed beneath him, diving steeply. There were just split seconds to fire, owing to the great speed of the fighters in their diving attacks.

The crew knew they had serious problems. There was a brief respite as the fighters readied for another attack. Some of the men watched as the German fighters climbed high behind them, readying for another attack. The men in the back of the plane knew their entire radio system was out, so there was no possibility of communication. Hickman watched from the tail turret as the fighters dove from above them in another steep attack. He was firing on one as it came in from above and slightly to his right. He could see hits on the plane, but this one wasn't scoring any hits on *Flak Shak*.

As Hickman fired a couple more short bursts, he felt the impact of shells hitting the back of the plane. They couldn't be from the ME-109 in his sights. He looked high above and saw another fighter firing. He later swore he could see a cannon shell coming towards him. He felt an impact, nearly knocking him from his turret. It felt like a hammer had hit him. Slowly he got his bearings and realized he had been hit on the top of his head by a cannon shell. He focused his eyes and looked up through the blood streaming down his forehead, seeing thin air above him. The top of his turret had been blown off and the cold wind was rushing in.

Caine, at the left waist gun, was wounded in this same attack, in his head, hand and leg. He fell to the floor of the plane, amidst the shell casings, bleeding badly. Shimer, at the right waist gun, was also hit with shrapnel, in the shoulder, back and arm. He stayed at his gun, continuing to shoot at the attacking planes.

Hickman tried to focus his eyes and saw bright colors flickering in the broken, jagged Plexiglas edges of his turret. He looked behind him into the body of the plane and saw blue flames, like a blow torch. One of the oxygen tanks behind Shimer's waist position had been hit by cannon or machinegun fire! He had to put the fire out before the entire bomber was engulfed in flames, so he disconnected the intercom, heated flying suit and oxygen lines, got out of his turret and worked his way past the oxygen tank, ducking beneath the flames. He felt weak and blood continued to drip from his head wound. He turned off the valve on the tank, but

Figure 24-S/Sgt. Martin Caine

that didn't stop the flames shooting out of it. The crew always carried a spare parachute in the back of the waist, so he picked up this parachute and held it against the oxygen tank, slowly smothering the fire.

Shimer had also seen the fire, but was unable to help, trying to fend off the fighters that were attacking from his side of the plane. He grabbed his parachute from the floor alongside him, snapped it on in case he had to bail out, and continued firing. Shimer saw Caine on the floor, but couldn't help him during these fighter attacks.[2]

When the fire was out, Hickman saw Caine lying on the floor in bad shape, bleeding from his head. Shimer was still firing as the fighters were attacking, but Hickman couldn't help Caine either. He had to get back to the tail turret to man his guns. He made his way the few short feet to the tail and got into the turret, just in time for another attack.

Another ME-109 came in from 6 o'clock high. He had it in his sights and opened up with a long burst, seeing the plane explode as it passed beneath him. There was a price to be paid and Hickman was hit again multiple times with shrapnel in subsequent attacks in the arms, legs and shoulder. He felt himself getting weak and knew he was in bad shape, but he couldn't do anything about it. Finally, he passed out, still sitting in the tail turret, manning his guns. (See Appendix A for Hickman injury summary.)

2nd Lt. Ben Barber's crew had seen *Flak Shak* fall out of the box and the crew watched as the plane fell farther behind. Barber decided to come to the aid of Wiggins' crew, whom he knew well from training, and pulled his bomber out the formation, descending rapidly. His thoughts were to take some of the pressure off and, as Barber's bomber descended, some of the German fighters focused their attention on Barber's plane with their diving attacks. Barber's crew would later claim four fighters destroyed, with only minor damage to their plane and no injuries to the crew.

To the men in *Flak Shak* it seemed like the attacks would never end. They watched some of the Messerschmitts attacking Barber's plane, but there were still several attacking them. The men lost track at the number of passes and the number of planes they had damaged. More holes appeared in the bomber after each pass. After more than a half hour, the remaining German fighters left, but *Flak Shak* still had to cross Yugoslavia and the Adriatic Sea if there was any hope of getting back to Italy.

As the attacks subsided Leasure got the first aid kit from the flight deck and made his way across the catwalk to the waist to treat the wounded. The three remaining Messerschmitts made a final frontal attack. Anderson hit one of them and saw smoke pouring from the engine as it dove away and soon the Germans were gone and there were only the two B-24's. Leasure had no idea of the carnage that he would find in the back of the plane.

Leasure found Caine on the floor by the left waist gun, a bloody mess, but conscious. Hickman was slumped over in the tail turret, unconscious, with blood streaming from his head. Shimer was also bleeding from several wounds, but still on his feet. Hartupee crawled out of the ball turret, with some minor shrapnel wounds, but in overall good shape. There were large holes in both sides of the plane, with bright daylight shining through.

Figure 25-Pvt. Robert Hickman

Figure 26-T/Sgt. Wilson Shimer

Leasure dragged Hickman from the tail turret, finding that he actually had several wounds. The head wound was the worst, so he found the spare parachute on the floor and tore it open, ripping pieces of the parachute to bandage Hickman's head and stop the bleeding. The other wounds weren't bleeding profusely, so next he went to help Hartupee, who was already working on Caine. They ripped more pieces of the parachute, along with bandages from the first aid kit, and stopped the major bleeding on Caine's head and right leg and gave him a shot of morphine.

Figure 27-Cpl.E. Hartupee   **Figure 28-S/Sgt. V. Anderson**

Anderson slid off the seat of the top turret after the last attack. He briefly spoke with both pilots. Wiggins had minor a minor shrapnel wound, but was OK. Hall had several shrapnel wounds, but refused treatment. Anderson went to the nose to check on Dempsey. He fashioned a splint for Dempsey's leg and decided to get him to the flight deck. Brittain helped and they carried and dragged Dempsey through the crawlway leading to the bomb bay, then lifted him onto the flight deck as carefully as possible, stretching him out behind the copilot's seat. After making Dempsey as comfortable as possible, Anderson made his way to the waist of the plane. He was aghast to find the men so badly wounded, with Leasure and Hartupee treating their wounds. He couldn't believe the damage he saw to the plane, with hydraulic fluid leaking from ruptured lines in the bomb bay and huge holes in the side of the aircraft.

Shimer made his way to the flight deck, ignoring his own wounds. Anderson also came forward again. There were some fuel leaks and both checked the fuel gauges. They agreed they might just have enough fuel to make it back to Italy if they could just keep flying, transferring fuel as necessary to keep the remaining engines working.

The plane, with all the damage to the control surfaces, was difficult to fly and both pilots had their hands full trying to maintain altitude, but gradually losing the battle. It seemed to take forever to make it to the Yugoslavian coast line, but finally they were over the Adriatic Sea. Alongside them was Barber's plane, their buddies. They couldn't communicate, since the radios were out, but it was still comforting to see them alongside.

Wiggins and Hall realized there was no possibility of bailing out, with several of the crew so seriously injured. If they couldn't make it, they'd have to ditch in the Adriatic Sea. The chances of a successful ditching in a B-24 were slim in the best of circumstances and these weren't the best circumstances. With the plane damaged so severely, it would be a miracle if they survived. With Barber's plane alongside, at least air/sea rescue could be alerted. Hall tore the right sleeve of his shirt off to check on the damage to his right arm, which was still bleeding. He saw several puncture wounds, but the bleeding had slowed. One of the gunners standing behind him on the flight deck helped him wrap bandages around his arm and he went back to the work of flying the plane with Wiggins.

Finally they approached the Italian coastline, but were still losing altitude. There was lots of tension inside the plane as the bomber sank lower and lower. With the hydraulics shot out they would have to crank the gear down. Shimer conferred with Anderson and they decided Anderson would crank the main gear down manually. Meanwhile, Shimer would crawl into the front of the pane and kick the nose gear out. Anderson started cranking as Shimer went to the nose. Both had just finished their tasks when they saw they were approaching land.

Wiggins spotted the airfield at Bari and headed for it. Shimer moved to his position between the pilots, calling out the airspeed. They were coming in fast, but Wiggins made a perfect landing. There was enough hydraulic fluid remaining for one application of the brakes, enough to stop the plane's roll at the end of the runway. The pilots swung the big bomber around and pointed it in the general direction of a parking area, killed the engines let the B-24 roll until it stopped.[3]

Almost immediately ambulances arrived to take the most seriously wounded away. These included Dempsey, Caine, Anderson, Hall and Shimer. The others were treated and released. Barber landed behind them and he took those who weren't hospitalized back to Venosa with him that night.

The next day the engineering officer for the 831st Sqdn, 1st Lt. Hank Dahlberg, came over to assess the damage to *Flak Shak*. He couldn't believe that the big bomber made it back from the target. The tail turret was nearly blown off the back of the plane and the top turret sustained major damage. Every major control surface had been hit, radios were shot out, the hydraulics were out, the trim tabs were shot away, several control cables were shot away, there was major damage to two engines, and all four propellers had been hit, The men counting the machinegun holes in the plane stopped when they reached 500. There were sixty two 20mm cannon holes throughout the plane. Dahlberg concluded the B-24 wasn't worth repairing. He returned a couple days later to remove the guns from the bomber and left *Flak Shak* to be scrapped.

Figure 29-note top of Hickman's tail turret

**Figure 30-Top turret with Plexiglas shattered
(Machinegun was removed after plane landed)**

Figure 29-Note bullet holes beneath cockpit windows

Figure 30-Frontal view with crew looking at damage

Figure 31-note damage to flaps

**Figure 32-Damage behind Shimer's position
(This is where oxygen tank caught fire.)**

Figure 33-Note cannon holes near Martin Caine's position

Hall's injuries were to his right arm, right side and right leg. The hospital initially located six holes, most of them small, and two additional puncture wounds were found while he was hospitalized. The day after his arrival he was already up and about, checking on his crewmates and writing letters home. He was released to return to the 485th Bomb Group several days later.[4]

Wiggins, Hall, Leasure, Hartupee, Brittain and Anderson were sent for a much needed rest to the Isle of Capri after Hall returned to Venosa in early July. By the middle of July most were again flying combat missions and Hall had been promoted to 1st lieutenant. Others also received promotions and Wiggins was promoted to captain. They got a new B-24, aptly named *Flak Shak II*. In early August the 831st Sqdn flight surgeon, Captain Johnson, grounded several of the crew, saying they were too nervous to fly combat. Within weeks most of the remaining crew members were reassigned, and flying with other crews. Hall flew several missions as an instructor pilot, flying with new crews on their first combat mission.[5]

The flight surgeon wanted to send the entire remaining crew home, but the powers that be in the group wanted the men to stay in Italy in a non-flying capacity if they couldn't fly combat. Hall wanted to be home with his wife to celebrate his 21st birthday in November so he chose to fly, as did the others, in order to complete the required missions. He probably expressed some of his thoughts about the mission best in a letter he wrote home. *"The old routine of having a war to fight sort of peps a man up 'til he gets shot in the process…then he begins to wonder."*[6]

Dempsey, Caine and Hickman required major surgery, due to the seriousness of their wounds. Hickman's medical report revealed that he had a compound, depressed skull fracture. His surgery was for "elevation of depressed fragments for skull fracture". Dempsey's and Caine's injuries were even more severe. Both were returned to the U.S. for further treatment. (See Appendix A for Hickman's medical summary.)

Shimer, in addition to the shrapnel injuries to his shoulder, back and arm, found more shrapnel in his foot while hospitalized. He would remain in the hospital for more than two months for treatment of his wounds. He returned to Venosa in mid-September and was kept on non-flying status, as a propeller specialist.[7]

One would have thought Hickman would have been sent home as well, but this was not the case, despite the serious injury to his head from the exploding cannon shell. He recovered substantially from his injuries and was considered well enough to return to the 485th base at Venosa in late August. When he returned he found his tent had been cleaned out and all his belongings, including his uniforms, were gone.

On September 2nd Hall was returning from flying a short hop to another base in Italy and, upon landing, was ordered to immediately report to the field for a presentation. He met the other six men from his crew who were now at the base: Wiggins, Leasure, Anderson, Brittain, Hickman and Hartupee. They were presented the Silver Star medal for their efforts on the June 28th mission. Dempsey, Caine and Shimer received their Silver Stars in the hospital. It was a rare occasion that an entire B-24 crew was awarded this medal. The citation says it all:

> *For gallantry in action as crew of a B-24 type aircraft. On 28 June 1944, this crew participated in a bombing mission against highly important and vital enemy oil fields in Rumania. Enroute to the target severe enemy opposition in the form of intense and accurate anti-aircraft fire and enemy fighters was encountered, inflicting grave damage to the aircraft this gallant crew was flying, and seriously wounding the bombardier. Despite the damaged condition of their aircraft and continued heavy enemy opposition, these men skillfully maintained their lead position, thereby completing a highly successful bombing run. The bombardier displayed great courage in releasing his bombs despite his severe wound. Rallying from the target their aircraft was savagely attacked by eight enemy fighters, who singled out their crippled aircraft and made seven aggressive attacks before being finally driven away. Despite the seriousness and almost uncontrollable condition of their aircraft these courageous crewmen remained at their stations and*

succeeded in warding off the enemy aircraft. Nine of these crew members were seriously wounded by enemy fire, but in the face of disaster destroyed six of the hostile aircraft. The pilot, co-pilot and navigator displayed great technique in pulling the aircraft out of a steep dive and bring it back to an advanced allied air field without the protection of other friendly aircraft. By their gallant action, firm determination to successfully complete their mission, and their sincere devotion to duty this gallant crew has upheld the highest tradition of the Military Service, thereby reflecting great credit upon themselves and the Armed Forces of the United States of America.[8]

**Figure 34-Front Row, Left to right: Leasure, Wiggins, Hall.
Back Row, Left to Right: Hartupee, Anderson, Brittain, Hickman**

Wiggins, Leasure, Anderson, and Hartupee eventually complete the required 50 missions and returned home. By the end of September Hickman was flying combat missions again with various crews who needed a fill-in gunner. He eventually completed 53 missions and returned to the U.S. in late December. Dempsey and Caine faced long recovery periods and Caine was in the hospital for nearly 1 ½ years.[9]

Matt Hall was not as fortunate. He wouldn't make it home to his wife for his 21st birthday. In fact, he was killed just 11 days after receiving his Silver Star. He was flying as a copilot with Captain

Figure 35-Matt Hall in cockpit

William Lawrence, another one of the original 485th pilots. On September 13, 1944 they were flying as deputy leader, bombing the synthetic oil refinery at Auschwitz, Poland. Several of the men were scheduled to complete their 50th mission that day, earning their ticket home, but it was not to be. The plane was hit by anti-aircraft fire over the target. Both pilots stayed at the controls of the plane to give the crew time to bail out. The pilots were last seen on the flight deck and their remains were later recovered from the crash site and buried by Polish farmers.[10]

NOTES AND REFERENCES

[1] In an interview in the July 1944 issue of *Bombs Away*, the 485th BG camp newsletter, pilot Wiggins described the first fighter attack as coming before the bombs were dropped. Radio Operator Caine said in a later World-telegram newspaper story, quoting a letter to his mother, that 8 Me-109's attacked them when they were approaching the target. The Silver Star citation indicates both fighters and anti-aircraft fire was encountered before the target. Tail gunner Hickman, in a 1/19/11, believed flak knocked out an engine on the bomb run. Flight engineer Shimer, thought a mechanical problem knocked out an engine on the bomb run. An undated press release for top turret gunner Anderson states that the first attack by ME-109's was over the target. I chose to use the information from interviews closest to when the incident occurred for this story.

[2] When I interviewed Shimer, he didn't realize that Hickman had put the fire out. He knew it had gone out, but was focused on the fighter attacks, and hadn't noticed Hickman fighting the fire.

[3] Shimer described his and Anderson's work to lower the gear in an interview with the author on 3/22/11. Hal described the landing and stopping of the plane in a 7/1/44 letter home.

[4] The two additional wounds were revealed in a letter Hall wrote home on 7/1/44, along with comments about his crewmates.

[5] Hall referenced the grounding in a letter home dated 8/2/44, along with the options given to him.

[6] Matt Hall letter home, dated 8/18/44.

[7] From author's interview with Shimer on 3/22/11.

[8] Taken from 15th Air Force General Order 3052, 9/2/44. See appendix B for copy of original document.

[9] For unknown reasons, Hickman flew more than the required 50 missions.

[10] The information about Hall on his last mission, regarding his position on the plane are from interviews with Dan Blodgett (1/25/04), Vernon Christensen, and Paul Canin (both interviewed by author on 1/15/04). These men were on Captain Lawrence's plane and survived the war as POWs. All three saw both pilots on the flight deck. The plane went into a spin after these three men got out. The author interviewed Stefan Wiktor in Zygodowice, Poland on 9/14/04. Wiktor was one of the farmers assisting in burying the airmen.

The Ivan Tyer Crew

James Scott woke up falling through the air, feet first. He must have been unconscious. As he regained his senses he realized he'd been blown out of the airplane. It had all happened so quickly. There was severe pain in his right hand. Looking down he saw that much of the flesh was missing. He also had a scalp wound that was bleeding profusely.[1] He looked down and saw he was very close to the ground. Scott still had his flak jacket on over his parachute and he pulled the emergency release, but the jacket wouldn't release.

The flak jacket was over his parachute and he had to do something quickly. He reached inside his flak jacket with his left hand and tried to pull the ripcord. He couldn't get to it. He managed to reach inside the flak jacket with his right hand, wrapped the injured fingers around the ripcord and pulled it hard enough to release the chute. The parachute partially deployed, but the shroud lines became entangled in the flak jacket. He frantically clawed at the jacket and it finally released and fell away. The parachute popped open with a jolt. Scott saw the intact tail of the plane fall past him, and it was at this point that Scott fully understood that the plane had exploded, blowing him out. Almost immediately after the chute deployed he hit the ground. The fuselage of *Nudist Kay* was burning nearby. Scott landed in a large grain field outside of Bucharest. Local farmers were in the field, cutting the grain with scythes.

Dazed, he tried to piece together what had happened. He remembered watching the big puffy clouds out the waist window, clouds so thick that he almost thought he could walk on them. He remembered that he and Peterson, the other waist gunner, snapped on their chest parachutes about the time they reached the I.P. Then he put on his flak jacket over the parachute. He remembered squeezing his oxygen mask to break off some of the ice particles inside the mask and it was then the flak started.

Figure 36-Front Row, Left to Right: 2nd Lt. Ivan Tyer, pilot; 2nd Lt. Milton Hirsch, navigator; 2nd Lt. Seymour Segan, bombardier and 2nd Lt. Richard Jordan, copilot. Back Row, Left to Right: Sgt. Webster Burrows, tail gunner; Sgt. Clayton Peterson, waist gunner; S/Sgt. Peter Buchanauer, nose gunner; Corporal Robert Anderson, top turret gunner; S/Sgt. James Scott, radio operator/waist gunner, and Sgt. Horace O'Connor, ball gunner.

A swarm of German fighters came through the flak, attacking from the 10 o'clock position. *Nudist Kay* was the last plane at the back of the first wave. They must have been hit by flak or fighters on the first pass because the #4 prop was a runaway, racing uncontrollably. The #2 prop was wind milling, just turning with the wind, its broad

The Ivan Tyer Crew

blades creating tremendous drag on that side of the plane. As they came off the bomb run the fighters attacked again, from six o'clock this time and the bomber fell out of the formation. The engines sounds were deafening to Scott. The intercom was knocked out. He got in several bursts from his machinegun as the fighters passed the waist, close enough that he could see the pilots' faces.

Scott knew they were in trouble and Peterson must have also sensed it. They both tried to make it to the camera hatch to bail out, but the plane went into a steep, almost vertical dive and they couldn't reach it. Looking back, he saw the entire bomb bay was on fire, shooting flames in his direction. He held onto his waist gun, trying to pull himself out the window, but couldn't get out. The centrifugal force had him pinned to the top of the plane. He knew he was going to die and his life passed before his eyes. Then, suddenly, he was free.

Others in the formation watched what happened to Tyer's plane. One of the observers was S/Sgt. Al Martin. Martin was a friend of Scott's, having trained with him and his crew before going overseas and was also in the 829th Sqdn. Al was the radio operator and left waist gunner in his aircraft. His crew was flying in the #2 position and he had a clear view of what happened behind them. He later recalled that the first fighter attack came in from 10 o'clock level. He managed to shoot off a short burst at some of the Messerschmitts as they dove past, above and below the formation, then looked out the window to see Scott's plane smoking.[2]

Figure 37-S/Sgt. Al Martin

Martin made a witness statement after he returned from the

mission that day, relating what he observed.

> *After the formation passed over the target, his ship was straggling, all engines were in operation, ship was losing altitude, smoke appeared from one engine. Landing gear was lowered, but raised when seven (7) fighters closed in and attacked, flak hit the ship, ship went into a spin, crashed and blew up. Two persons bailed out, one chute definitely opened, and the other may have, however aircraft was very low at this time.*[3]

Now back in the present, standing in the grain field, Scott heard the sound of a plane engine above him. He looked up and saw a ME-109 lining up on him. The plane had a red spinner on the nose. He assumed he was going to be strafed so he hugged the ground, trying to make himself as small a target as possible. The pilot made a low pass over him, but didn't shoot.

Scott looked around him and saw that he was now surrounded by those farmers who had been working in the field. Some of them held double-barrel shotguns. There was no way he was going to escape. The Rumanians were trying to communicate with him. They apparently thought he was Russian, so he kept saying "Americano" to let them know he was an American. While trying to communicate with them he took off his flying coveralls, leaving only his khaki uniform which had no insignias. His clothes were covered in blood from the injuries to his hand and head.

He looked off in the distance and saw another American airman a few hundred yards away. He correctly assumed that it was one of his fellow crewmen. A Rumanian officer arrived and put a Luger pistol against his temple, motioning for him to put his hands up. Despite his injuries, he complied. After a few minutes this officer let him walk over to the other airman. It was his bombardier, 2nd Lt. Seymour Segan was in bad shape and in extreme pain, with a compound fracture of his right leg. The leg was resting on the piled up nylon from Segan's parachute, causing him even more pain. Scott tried to explain to the group surrounding him that this sitting position for

Segan was very painful. They didn't pay any attention. Finally, Scott grabbed one of the men by his collar, pulling him backwards and the man fell on the ground.

Another farmer was on a big white stallion. He seemed to be the leader or boss of these farmers and he wasn't happy about Scott's actions. The farmer charged him on the horse and the horse reared up, then came down, trying to paw him. Scott managed to sidestep the horses' hooves. The farmer tried this tactic several times, but Scott was able to stay away from the horse's feet.

Some of the other farmers pointed in a different direction and tried to make Scott understand that there was another airman nearby. Finally he understood what they were trying to tell him. The spot they pointed to was several hundred yards away, but the farmers wouldn't let him go and see this airman. Scott assumed it was Peterson, and that he was dead, since Peterson was in the same part of the plane and it would make sense that he would be nearby if he was thrown from the plane.[4]

Soon a small twin-engine German plane landed in the field. There were two men in the plane, both Rumanian military, a pilot and a radio operator. The pilot spoke perfect English and told them he and Segan would be going with him. They carried Segan to the plane, and all four of them flew to an airport on the outskirts of Bucharest. Scott guessed the grain field in which he had landed was about 50 miles west of Bucharest.

Segan was taken to a hospital, due to his serious leg injury. When they separated Scott wondered whether they'd ever meet again. He was escorted into a small building at the airport, where there were several German pilots. One of the pilots stood beside him and began an interrogation. This pilot had a riding crop in his hand, an apparent attempt to show that he was the boss, the ranking officer. The pilot handed him a card that asked for his name, rank and serial number. There were additional questions about his plane, his base and other details about his service that he didn't intend to answer. Although his right hand was injured, he managed to write down his name, rank and serial number, but didn't answer the other questions. The pilot realized he wasn't going to get any additional information and called for two Rumanian guards to take Scott away.

The two Rumanian guards were armed with submachine guns. They marched him all around the area, showing him the damage allegedly caused that day by the bombing. The only English words the guards seemed to know were "murderer" and "gangster" and they called him these names repeatedly as they walked around, one of them holding a gun barrel against his back. After a lengthy walk they arrived at a large building with a courtyard. He saw soldiers with rifles approaching from the building. They entered the building and Scott was ordered up a flight of stairs and then locked in a small room.

About an hour later the guard returned, motioned for him to get up and pointed for him to go out the door, again putting a gun barrel in his back. They went down the stairs and outside. A car drove up and stopped, Scott was pushed into the back seat and it sped off. He had no idea what was happening. They drove for quite a while, stopped along a large street and Scott was ordered out of the car. He and his guard were quickly approached by a crowd of civilians, who yelled and spit at him. Once again their vocabulary contained the words "murderer" and "gangster". Some made motions with their hands, indicating they wanted to slit his throat. The guard ordered him onto a crowded streetcar. The civilians on the streetcar continued to harangue him, but he just stood there quietly.

Scott just didn't care anymore. It had been a very long day, first flying a combat mission, being blown out of a plane that was destroyed by flak and fighters, dodging a horse trying to trample him, flying in a German plane, walking around a bombed out city, riding to parts unknown in a car, and now riding in this streetcar with people calling him names. He was wounded, in pain and had lost a great deal of blood. He guessed that most of his buddies from the crew were dead. Just how much worse could it get?

He was taken off the streetcar by his guard, again at gunpoint, and was forced to walk through the streets. Locals began to gather, following him and again began yelling and calling him names. The crowd grew and soon there were nearly 300 angry civilians. At this point he was glad to have the guard with the gun barrel in his back. The guard could protect him from this mob, if need be.

After walking several blocks they reached a large building, surrounded by a high fence. He was taken inside the fenced area and a man approached, wearing part of an Air Force uniform, and identified himself as Major Yeager. This was a prison and Yeager said he was the senior ranking officer in the camp, run by the Rumanians. Yeager began asking him all kinds of questions about the war. Scott was unsure of whether or not Yeager was who he claimed to be, so he told the officer he didn't want to answer any questions. He was tired and just wanted to rest. He could tell that Yeager didn't like him, but it didn't really matter.

Two Rumanian soldiers took him to a room and had him undress. They thoroughly searched him and then had him get into a large wooden tub filled with warm water. One of the Rumanian soldiers scrubbed him. It felt good and got rid of most of the caked blood. They also washed his khaki uniform, getting off most of the blood stains.

He thought he was seeing a ghost a few days later when 2nd Lt. Milton Hirsch arrived at the camp. Hirsch was the navigator from his crew and it was good to learn there was another survivor. Sadly, no other survivors from the crew showed up. Scott was at this camp for several days. He was in the officer's POW camp and he and three other enlisted men were unceremoniously taken to the enlisted men's POW camp, where the conditions were not as good.[5]

The new camp was on a hospital grounds. This was a big disadvantage for the prisoners in that it was only three blocks from the main railroad marshaling yard, a primary target for allied bombers. Scott noted the conditions were much different than the officer's camp. Rank apparently had its privileges. On August 23, 1944 Rumania switched sides as the Russians approached and joined the allies. The prisoners were released, but they were not out of danger, since the Germans were still in the area. German planes strafed and bombed the city for several days, a particularly dangerous situation for the POWs.

In early September Scott was airlifted out of Rumania and taken back to Italy with more than 1100 fellow POWs. He returned home to the U.S. and spent 4 months in the hospital being treated for combat injuries and illnesses brought on while a POW.

NOTES AND REFERENCES

[1] He later realized the wound wasn't severe.
[2] Info from author's 3/29/11 phone interview with Al Martin.
[3] Martin's Witness Statement from MACR 6410.
[4] Scott never learned the identity of the other dead airman.
[5] In Scott's unpublished memoir he maintained that he had run afoul of Major Yaeger and this was the reason for the transfer. Scott's account of what happened came from that unpublished memoir.

The John Crouchley Crew

The first wave dropped their bombs on the first alternate target and the second wave was just far enough behind them that the lead bombardier in the second wave could make out the primary target through the clouds. 2nd Lt. Crouchley's bomber, hindered by engine mechanical problems, was having difficulty keeping up with the formation. It had moved back from the #5 position to the #7 position, Tail-End Charlie, in the lead box. Just after they dropped their bombs, ME-109 fighters attacked from above. T/Sgt. William Peters, a waist gunner in the plane flying deputy lead in the #2 position, had a ringside seat and witnessed what happened next.

Figure 38-T/Sgt. William Peters

> *While over the target I saw ship 701 (Crouchley's plane) was hit three times by fighters firing twenty millimeter shells, once in the wing near number 3 engine and twice in the waist directly under the right waist window and the upper left of the window.*
>
> *At this time, Number 2 and 3 engines caught fire at approximately 22,000 feet altitude. The ship started lagging behind and losing altitude, then started*

into a dive of about 30 to 40 degrees, (in my opinion trying to put out the fires), and was then attacked by six ME-109's coming in from 4 to 7 o'clock high. At last sight, ship was still losing altitude. It is estimated that at last sight, the ship was at about 10,000 feet, and seemed to be increasing in speed and steepness of dive.

I saw no parachutes, nor was any movement seen near the waist windows. The ME-109's were still hovering about the crippled ship, and it is therefore assumed that the ship went down without regaining level flight. [1]

Figure 39-Front Row, Left to Right: 2nd Lt. John Crouchley; 2nd Lt. Allen Meister, bombardier; 2nd Lt. Forrest Leveille, navigator; 2nd Lt. William Hays, copilot. Back Row, Left to Right: S/Sgt. Ralph Perillo, waist gunner; Sgt. Thomas Langstaff, waist gunner; Sgt. Edward Johnson, ball gunner; Sgt. Eugene LaScotte, nose gunner; S/Sgt. Donald Turner, top turret gunner, and Sgt. William Van Meer, tail gunner.

But the bomber didn't go down. Another observer saw a cannon shell strike the fuselage along the copilot's position on the right side of the plane. It was much more personal inside the plane. In the nose turret LaScotte didn't see the planes in the first attack, but felt the concussion of cannon shells exploding behind him. He heard someone call out over the intercom "Fighters at 2 o'clock level!", and immediately felt and heard explosions somewhere behind the nose turret. They fell farther behind the formation, now an easy target for the German fighters. The entire formation made a right turn, heading west, while Crouchley's plane continued south, still losing altitude.²

One shell that LaScotte heard came through the bomber's windshield, exploding behind the pilots. Another came through the instrument panel, destroying some of the instruments, including the compass. Another pierced the side of the plane, adjacent to the copilot, spraying Lt. Hays with bits of shrapnel.³

Figure 40-Sgt. Thomas Langstaff

After the formation had left them, still headed west, they crossed the Danube River into Bulgaria. The plane continued to lose power and altitude and the fighter attacks continued from behind. Sgt. Ed Johnson was in the ball turret, firing at the attacking fighters. Both waist gunners were wounded in the first fighter attack. Sgt. Thomas Langstaff had 64 pieces of shrapnel in him and S/Sgt. Ralph Perillo was riddled with 40 pieces of shrapnel from the exploding cannon shells. Both were out of action and lying on the floor of the plane. Johnson's oxygen was knocked out, along with the intercom system to the back of the plane.⁴

In the tail turret, S/Sgt. William Van Meer had his hands full. While he was firing at an attacking fighter (there were six in this group), a 20mm cannon shell came through the turret, knocking off the oxygen regulator and struck a glancing blow on his flak helmet, injuring him, but luckily not exploding.⁵ As the fighters continued their attacks from the rear, Van Meer fired again, hit one and watched it dive steeply beneath the bomber, smoking. Johnson fired at it as it passed, from his position in the ball turret, seeing it go down. It passed from his view before it hit the ground.

Cannon fire from one of the attackers hit the ammunition chute carrying the .50 caliber ammo belts in the back of the B-24 to the tail turret, jamming the flow of ammunition, making the tail guns useless, since the bullets couldn't get to either gun. Johnson felt himself getting weak from the loss of oxygen as the plane went into a steep dive. The oxygen system had also been knocked out in the rear of the plane. Because they were in a steep dive and descending quickly, he

Figure 41-S/Sgt. William Van Meer

Figure 42-S/Sgt. Donald Turner

didn't lose consciousness. Now his guns and the guns from the top turret gunner/engineer S/Sgt. Donald Turner were the only guns that could fire rearward and their field of vision was limited by the double tail assembly and fuselage. When they finally leveled out, Van Meer, who had a head wound, got out of his tail turret to render assistance to the injured waist gunners.

For much of the time only one of Johnson's two ball turret guns was firing, thereby keeping him in ammunition for the entire battle. The fighters made repeated attacks from the rear and came so close that it was difficult to miss them. Johnson scored hits on several of the fighters as they dove beneath the bomber, watching two of them go

The John Crouchley Crew

down, in addition to the victory he already shared with Van Meer.

Turner, in the top turret, continued to fire his guns at the five or six fighters that remained, even after the top of his turret was shattered by cannon fire. Turner thought two of the aircraft he hit went down, but it was difficult for him to tell because the attacks continued, fast and furious. Turner's and Johnson's guns remained the only ones protecting the back of the plane and this is where all the attacks came. Since the tail guns were useless and there were blind spots for both gunners if the attackers came in level, the Germans had a huge advantage in their continuing attacks.[6]

The bomber was in bad shape, with two engines out, gas lines ruptured and hydraulic fluid leaking from the lines, severed by shell fragments. The plane was heading farther south into Bulgaria, alone and with no possibility of getting help. The intercom system in the front of the plane was working, but there was no communication with those in the back of the plane.

Navigator Wilson's compasses had been shot out, so he couldn't give the pilots a precise heading. They were headed generally in a SSW direction. They weren't lost, but they didn't know their precise location in Bulgaria at this point. Wilson could do little except watch for attacking fighters and point them out to the others in the front of the plane on the intercom.[7]

Figure 43-2nd Lt. John Wilson

One engine was out, one was still on fire and one was spinning uncontrollably. The bomber continued to lose altitude and speed. LaScotte felt helpless up in the nose turret. The attacks were all from the rear. He looked back, over the navigator's astrodome that was directly behind and above his turret. From this position he could see above the B-24 and could see the fighter attacks if they came behind and were high enough above the plane. He saw Lt. Wilson watching him through the small window in the closed door of the turret. Wilson was being thrown about the plane, because it was bucking and shaking. The Messerschmitts made diving turns either to the left or right after raking the bomber from above with gunfire. If the planes didn't dive away too steeply, LaScotte quickly turned around and got off a few shots as they passed in front of his turret. He hit one and saw the tail break off as it passed beneath and in front of him. He didn't continue watching, because they were still under attack.[8]

During a brief lull in the attacks LaScotte heard the pilot call to the bombardier, 2nd Lt. Hollowell, telling him to check on the men in the back of the plane. Someone also called for morphine, saying that two men were hit. Hollowell got morphine from a first aid kit and took it to the back of the plane. The narrow catwalk was dripping with the slippery hydraulic fluid from ruptured lines along the walls of the bomb bay, making Hollowell's passage even more hazardous than usual. The plane was pitching and rolling, but smoothed out when Crouchley finally got the fire out in one of the engines and feathered the propeller on the runaway engine.

Figure 44-Sgts. LaScotte and Johnson

As the plane lumbered on its course, losing altitude, the frequency of the attacks subsided. LaScotte looked off to his left and spotted an ME-109 alongside of them, slowly edging into his view, just a few hundred yards away, traveling just a little faster than the bomber. As the plane slowly eased ahead of them, LaScotte managed to get his guns turned and fired a short burst at the plane. Just as he fired the plane pitched violently and Crouchley yelled over the intercom, "What the hell are you doing, Scotty? That's a P-51!" LaScotte answered, "It might be a P-51, but he's shooting the hell out of us." Crouchley responded, "Well, get him then." The Messerschitt had already dived beneath and came up behind the bomber, gaining altitude and made a diving pass from behind. LaScotte managed to get a short burst off as the plane dove out of sight, apparently unharmed.[9]

Several minutes passed without any further attacks. LaScotte crawled out of the nose turret to check on his buddies in the back of the plane. They were still losing altitude fairly rapidly and the engines were running rough. He snapped on his chest parachute that he had left outside his turret and crawled along the nose wheel on his hands and knees until he got to the bomb bay, then climbed up onto the flight deck. Over the loud noise of the engines he yelled to the pilot, asking "What are our chances?" Crouchley told him they were in bad shape. He couldn't let loose of the controls without the plane going into a spin and they couldn't maintain altitude with the two damaged engines. They were also losing fuel from the ruptured tanks and Crouchley estimated they only had ten or fifteen minutes of fuel left before they had to bail out. He said he'd try to get them over Yugoslavia before the bail-out, where they might have a chance of being picked up by friendly Partisans. Turner was on the flight deck, keeping a close eye on the fuel gauges that were on the bulkhead leading to the bomb bay. Wilson was standing behind the pilots on the flight deck.

Meanwhile, in the ball turret, Johnson felt a bumping on the back of his turret. There were no planes attacking so he rotated his turret downward so he could open the hatch and find out what was causing the bumping. It was Van Meer, standing in the well for the ball turret, banging on the hatch with his flak helmet. He yelled at Johnson to get out of his turret, saying the bailout bell had sounded, warning the crew to prepare to jump. The bell couldn't be heard inside the ball turret and, since the intercom was out in the back of the plane, there was no other way to warn Johnson.

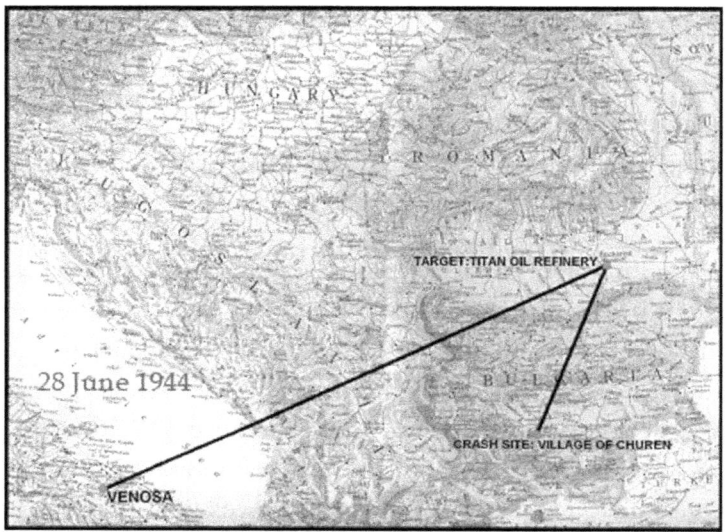

Figure 45-Flight path of Crouchley's plane

Johnson climbed out of the turret, stretched his legs and stood up. As he climbed over the well (the support system for the turret) he looked around inside the plane for the first time. It was a mess. Langstaff and Perillo, the two waist gunners, were lying wounded on the floor of the plane. There were shell holes, some of them the size of a man's head on the sides of the plane, visible reminders of the ongoing battle with the enemy. He looked out the waist window and saw more holes in the wings, one of them big enough for a man to crawl through.

Since Johnson had been wearing only his heated G.I. booties in the ball turret, he began to remove them, intending to put on his G.I. shoes before bailing out. He knew he didn't have much time before the bell would sound again, the signal to leave the plane. As he was changing his shoes, another Messerschmitt attacked and shrapnel from an exploding cannon shell struck him in the side. He fell to the floor on his face, just lying there, wondering how badly he was wounded. He learned later that Van Meer and the others thought he was dead.

Van Meer jumped up, ran to the waist window, and looked out. The fighter that made the attack was flying alongside them, looking them over, about 50 feet away, probably wondering how they could still be flying. Van Meer aimed the waist gun at the ME-109, an easy target, and shot him down with a long burst. Johnson got up, despite the pain in his side and put his shoes on. Then he got a bandage from a nearby first aid kit and put it on the wound, inside his flight suit.

LaScotte had made his way across the slippery catwalk in the bomb bay to check on his buddies in the back of the plane after checking in with the pilot. Gasoline lines and hydraulic lines were ruptured and both fluids dripped from the metal tubing. The smell of the fluids was strong. Since all communications were out in the back of the plane, LaScotte made his way back across the catwalk, planning to get forward to the flight deck.

LaScotte was standing on the catwalk, holding onto bomb shackles for balance, when the bomb bay doors opened. He looked toward the front of the plane, realizing that Turner had opened the doors. Turner yelled "Jump!" LaScotte turned around on the catwalk to see if those in the back of the plane had gotten the word. Apparently they had, as he saw the wounded waist gunners, Perillo and Langstaff, being pushed out of the plane through the camera hatch by other crew members.

Johnson sat at the camera hatch, legs dangling out, ready to jump, and looked down. He saw a sheepherder looking up at him, less than 500 feet below. Then he jumped. Several seconds later Hollowell jumped through the hatch. Van Meer was last out through the hatch.

Turner and LaScotte, being good buddies, had always said they would jump together if they ever had to bail out. LaScotte turned around on the catwalk to face the front of the plane. Turner was gone!

He saw a figure standing on the flight deck above him. It was Wilson. He yelled, "Where are we?" Wilson answered, "Yugoslavia!" Behind Wilson, Hays, the copilot, was walking to the bomb bay from his seat. LaScotte jumped. A few seconds later Wilson jumped, followed by Hays.[10]

While the plane was under attack, it was the middle of the night in Minnesota, several hours earlier. Eugene LaScotte's uncle Ray awakened in the early morning hours, at 2 o'clock. He had broken out in a cold sweat and had a terrible feeling that something bad had just happened to one of his three nephews who were in the service. He wrote down the time and tried to go back to sleep. In the morning he phoned LaScotte's mother to tell her of his feeling and to ask if she'd heard anything about her sons. She had experienced similar feelings, but wasn't sure it meant anything. Eugene LaScotte apparently wasn't the only one to have those feelings.[11]

Due to the low altitude, Turner pulled the ripcord on his parachute as soon as he cleared the bottom of the plane. It opened with a snap, he swung in a wide arc once and smacked into the ground. He landed on his back, with his left arm beneath him. The impact caused him to lose all sensation in that arm, and it didn't return for three months.

Turner had been told in an earlier briefing to go to the poorer class of people in hostile territory for help, because they'd be more likely to give assistance. He found the sheepherder he had seen just before he jumped and walked across the field to him. Turner gave him the bandage he put in his flight suit before the bail out and the man bandaged the wound in his side for him. The sheepherder led him to a small community nearby where there were four or five houses. Bulgarian soldiers soon arrived and took him into custody. That was the end of his freedom.

LaScotte's parachute opened with a snap and jerked so hard it knocked the wind out of him. He heard shots being fired from the ground, but didn't see the shooter. His bomber crashed into the side of a mountain about a half mile away. The parachute barely had time to open before he hit the ground, landing on his feet in a potato patch. He broke some toes on his right foot and fractured his left heel. There was no one nearby, so he hid his parachute and .45 pistol and began hobbling away from the area where he landed. The injuries to his feet were painful, but he needed to keep walking in order to get as far away from his landing site as he could and as quickly as possible.

After walking some distance he found a mountain stream. He stepped in the water and it seemed to soothe the pain in his feet, so he continued walking in the stream for a couple of hours. He had seen no one from the crew and had no idea where they were. He only knew that his plane hit the side of the mountain across the valley. He had no idea where he was going, but he kept walking.

About five hours after bailing out LaScotte heard voices and then a bullet whizzed past his head. He turned and saw Bulgarian soldiers in the distance. They had spotted him and fired. They had guns; he was unarmed. There were several of them; there was one of him. They were able-bodied; he could barely walk. It was an easy choice to surrender and he threw up his arms before they could shoot again. The guards marched him to a small town and they entered a small hotel. It was a hot day and the soldiers gave him a couple of beers.

Wilson jumped from the bomb bay after LaScotte, immediately pulling the ripcord on his parachute due to the low altitude. As he hung in his parachute, shots rang out from the valley below and he was hit in the leg by a rifle bullet, fired by a Bulgarian soldier. When he landed the Bulgarian soldier approached and aimed at him again, but the bolt jammed in the rifle, likely saving his life. The Bulgarian soldier took him prisoner instead of killing him.[12]

Figure 46-2nd Lt. Bill Hollowell   **Figure 47-2nd Lt. William Hays**

Hollowell broke both his legs upon landing. He was immediately captured and later taken to a nearby hospital for treatment. The others were quickly rounded up, except for Hays, who was the last to jump. He managed to elude his captors for a few days, but was eventually picked up when he went to a farmhouse for food and assistance.

The pilot, 2nd Lt. Crouchley never made it out of the plane. He was last seen by Hays, still at the controls, keeping the plane flying level so the others could get out.[13]

Most of the crew were taken to a civilian jail in Sofia and then taken by train to a POW camp at Shumen, arriving at different times. Hollowell was hospitalized with serious leg injuries and was the last to arrive at Shumen on August 25th.[14]

When the men first arrived there was a severe water shortage and the prisoners were limited to one quart of water per day. Food was also in short supply, both for the POWs and the civilian population. Most of the Bulgarians were unaware of the Geneva convention, as was evidenced in a later investigation into the mistreatment of POWs in Bulgaria. Many of the POWs reported harsh treatment before they arrived at the camp at Shumen, but camp life at Shumen wasn't any worse than any of the other Axis POW camps, aside from the food shortage.[15]

The senior ranking officer in the camp was Major Walter Smith. Major Smith was a pilot from the 485th, although the men from Crouchley's camp didn't know him. In late August 1944, the Russians were nearing the Bulgarian border. Bulgaria, although allied with Germany, claimed neutrality with Russia. The Russians demanded unconditional surrender. While negotiations were occurring, Major Smith arranged with the camp commandant to fly to Sofia and arrange the safe release of all Allied POWs in Bulgaria, along with their safe return to Allied territory. Even though the Bulgarians were joining the Allies, the Germans were still in Bulgaria and a great deal of fighting was yet to be done. The POWs in Shumen were in danger of getting caught up in the fighting.

A plan was agreed upon whereby the POWs would leave by train. In the early morning hours of September 9, 1944 the nine men from Crouchley's crew were loaded into trucks and taken to the train station, along with 282 other American POWs and 38 POWs of other nationalities. They boarded a train which took them into Turkey and then into Syria. Major Smith met them along the way to accompany them to freedom. From Syria the men were flown to Cairo, Egypt and then back to Italy and finally, they were sent home. For them, June 28th had been a very long mission.

Figure 48-After liberation

NOTES AND REFERENCES

[1] From written witness statement of T/Sgt. William H. Peters, MACR 6820

[2] LaScotte's information and personal observations were chronicled in a July 1944 letter home from the POW camp at Shumen, Bulgaria, along with four letters he wrote to John Wilson Jr. on 9/1/88, 11/2/88, 1/11/89 and 4/10/89, and a written debriefing statement he made after his return from captivity, included in MACR 6820.

[3] The details about the shell explosions in the cockpit are from a letter written by Ed Johnson to John Wilson Jr. on 9/28/88 and from the mission summary of the 485th BG mission that day. In the same letter Johnson supplied the details of his own experience and what he observed inside the plane when he left his turret.

[4] The details regarding the flak wounds to the waist gunners are also from Johnson's 9/28/88 letter to Wilson.

[5] MACR 6820 includes a statement from Perillo, attesting to Van Meer's head injury.

[6] Turner's information also came from Ed Johnson in the letter written to John Wilson Jr. on 9/28/88.

[7] Wilson's information is from his son, John Jr., who shared the info with the author in an email letter on 7/7/14

[8] In LaScotte's 7/28/88 interview with Dianne LaScotte he said Lt. Hollowell revealed in prison camp that he saw this plane hit the ground.

[9] The quotes came from Eugene LaScotte's letter to John Wilson Jr, dated 4/11/89.

[10] They actually were still in Bulgaria.

[11] This was revealed in an interview with Eugene LaScotte by Dianne LaScotte on July 28, 1988 and further documented in a story about LaScotte and his crew in 2005 written by Mary Albrecht. The family didn't receive the telegram advising of his Missing In Action status, for another week. LaScotte had two brothers in the service. One was a Navy pilot and the other was an Army Air Force pilot.

[12] This information came from the email letter sent by John Wilson Jr. on 7/7/14.

[13] From Witness Statement in MACR 6820

[14] The statistics about the Shumen camp, including numbers of prisoners and Hollowell's arrival date, are from Bob Johnson's book *gidi gidi boom boom*.

[15] The investigation into possible atrocities against American airmen held at the Shumen camp and in other parts of Bulgaria began shortly after the prisoners were freed and was headed by General William Hall. It was termed the Hall Mission and several of the recently freed POWs returned to Bulgaria to assist and identifying and apprehending those accused of atrocities. Major Walter Smith was one of those who returned. Lt. Colonel Baldridge, the operations officer for the mission, concluded no atrocities occurred involving Americans in the custody of Bulgarians. Some would disagree with his finding.

7

A Broader Picture

The 485th Bomb Group lost three B-24 bombers on the June 28th mission in a running battle that lasted more than a half an hour. Several others were severely damaged. There are no official records for some of the events that happened to other crews.

For example, Captain Roger Nichols, an 828th Squadron pilot, was in another B-24 that was heavily damaged on the mission, also over Bucharest. There were repeated fighter attacks on his plane, including one that left a hole the size of a man's head just inches from a waist gunner, but didn't injure him. There was damage to all four engines. Four of the main fuel cells were hit and many of the control cables were damaged. The bombardier was 2nd Lt. Tony Shulas. With oxygen shot out at many of the stations, Shulas kept busy delivering portable oxygen bottles to the different stations so the men could breathe at high altitude. This plane limped back to Venosa.

Figure 49-Captain Roger Nichols crew

With the damage to the hydraulic system, the flaps could not be lowered. Nichols brought the plane in to land at 150 mph, flying speed. Fortunately, the landing gear and tires held up and the plane made a safe landing. Yes, there are many such stories, some told and some untold, accounts never recorded in the official USAAF history.[1]

One would think the losses would be high in the other groups as well. After all, there were groups both ahead of and behind the 485th, a total of 229 B-24's assigned to bomb targets in Bucharest and an additional 138 planes assigned to bomb the Karlova, Bulgaria airfield.

The bomb group mission reports tell a different story. None of the other three groups in the 55th Bomb Wing lost any planes on this mission to either fighters or flak, not one single loss. Not one of the three bomb groups in the 49th Bomb Wing lost any aircraft and there were no losses from the four groups in the 304th Bomb Wing that bombed the Bulgarian airfield. The 485th had the only combat losses on this day, June 28, 1944.

The 465th Bomb Group led the mission for the entire 15th Air Force and was the first over Bucharest, dropping their bombs at 9:47AM. They encountered a total of five enemy planes (one JU-88, two ME-109's and two FW-190's). They reported destroying one ME-109 and one FW-190, while suffering no losses, all in the target area.[2]

The 464th Bomb Group followed the 465th over Bucharest and dropped their bombs at 9:48AM. They reported seeing German fighters in the target area doing aerobatics, but not one of them attacked their group. This was just four minutes before the 485th dropped their bombs.[3]

In the case of the 460th Bomb Group, which was behind the 485th, they dropped their bombs at 9:56AM, just four minutes after the 485th. A total of ten ME-109's attacked the group just after they dropped their bombs and not en masse. On their return to base, the 460th reported they shot down two of the attackers, with no damage to any of the B-24s from fighters. They reported ten aircraft had flak damage, but there were no reports of damage from the fighter attacks. The 460th also reported that they had P-51 escort cover in the target area, which undoubtedly was a deterrent to the enemy planes.[4]

The three bomb groups from the 49th Bomb Wing were several minutes behind the 55th Bomb Wing. Their target was in a different section of Bucharest, the Chitila Marshalling Yard. All three of these groups reported encounters with enemy fighters in the target area, but fewer bombers were attacked. The encounters weren't as intense and were at or near the target. It's likely that the presence of American P-51 fighters made a difference. In fact, the 451st Bomb Group mission narrative indicates the German fighters were driven off by the P-51's. One B-24 from the 461st Bomb Group reported slight damage from the attacking ME-109's, just that one aircraft slightly damaged by fighters of the three bomb groups in the entire bomb wing. Just a few planes in this wing suffered minor flak damage.[5]

The three planes from the 485th Bomb Group were shot down in a running battle that lasted more than 30 minutes. There were 30 airmen on the three planes. Nine of the men became POWs in Bulgaria; three were prisoners in Rumania, and 18 were killed. At least 12 men on the returning planes were wounded. Most of those captured were also wounded. (See list at end of chapter)

The German records reveal that German pilots claimed thirteen B-24's were shot down over Bucharest that day. Rumanian records indicate Rumanian pilots claimed one B-24 was and two B-17's were shot down over Bucharest. (The Rumanians were flying IAR 80's and IAR 81's, a single-engine fighter.) Official 15th Air Force records reveal that no B-17's were on combat missions that day in this region, so it's possible the B-24's were mistaken for B-17's. It's also probable that most of these claims were actually claims for the three 485th B-24's that went down, along with the two heavily damaged planes that landed at Bari. We know for a fact that there were only three losses.[6]

There were several factors that contributed to what happened to the 485th that day. The inbound escorts taking them to the target left when they believed their relief, the P-51's providing cover over the target had arrived, when they actually wouldn't arrive for another 15 minutes. The 485th was 10 minutes early, and their scheduled escorts were 10 minutes late. This was a time of war when things rarely go precisely as planned. This still doesn't explain why the 485th was singled out, but such was the fate of the 485th Bomb Group that day. What we do know is how the 485th Bomb Group reacted under attack and their story has now been told.

485th Bomb Group losses on June 28, 1944

Name	Position	Crew	Fate
1st Lt. Robert Sloan	pilot	Sloan	KIA
2nd Lt. Wallace Herzfeldt	copilot	Sloan	KIA
2nd Lt. Harry Pritchard	navigator	Sloan	KIA
2nd Lt. Robert Pumplin	bombardier	Sloan	KIA
S/Sgt. Joseph DeMaster	eng/waist gunner	Sloan	KIA
S/Sgt. Nathan Iacobacci	radio op/waist gunner	Sloan	KIA
S/Sgt. Robert Sinclair	ball gunner	Sloan	KIA
Sgt. Charles Buszinski	nose gunner	Sloan	KIA
Sgt. William Nigle	tail gunner	Sloan	KIA
Sgt. Glenn Shaw	top turret gunner	Sloan	KIA
2nd Lt. Ivan Tyer	pilot	Tyer	KIA
2nd Lt. Richard Jordan	copilot	Tyer	KIA
2nd Lt. Milton Hirsch	navigator	Tyer	POW
2nd Lt. Seymour Segan	bombardier	Tyer	POW
T/Sgt. Clayton Peterson	eng/waist gunner	Tyer	KIA
T/Sgt. James Scott	radio op/waist gunner	Tyer	POW
S/Sgt. Webster Burrows	tail gunner	Tyer	KIA
S/Sgt. Peter Buchanauer	nose gunner	Tyer	KIA
Sgt. Robert Anderson	top turret gunner	Tyer	KIA

Pvt. Horace O'Connor	ball gunner	Tyer	KIA
2nd Lt. John Crouchley	pilot	Crouchley	KIA
2nd Lt. William Hays	copilot	Crouchley	POW
2nd Lt. John Wilson	navigator	Crouchley	POW
2nd Lt. William Hollowell	bombardier	Crouchley	POW
S/Sgt. Donald Turner	eng/top turret gunner	Crouchley	POW
S/Sgt. William Van Meer	radio op/tail gunner	Crouchley	POW
Sgt. Edward Johnson	ball gunner	Crouchley	POW
S/Sgt. Ralph Perillo	waist gunner	Crouchley	POW
Sgt. Thomas Langstaff	waist gunner	Crouchley	POW

NOTES AND REFERENCES

[1] Nichols described the damage in a 6/29/44 letter home to his parents. See Appendix D for letter.
[2] 465th Bomb Group narrative mission report for 6/28/44.
[3] 464th Bomb Group narrative mission report for 6/28/44.
[4] 460th Bomb Group narrative mission report for 6/28/44.
[5] 451, 451st and 461st narrative mission reports for 6/28/44.
[6] The source of the Rumanian information is Sandra Oprescu, Rumanian historian and an ex-wife of Rumanian fighter ace Dan Vizanty. She obtained the claims from Rumanian military records. The German information is from Tony Wood's Combat Claims and Casualty List.

Epilogue

So the war ended. The premonitions both LaScotte and Scott had before that fateful mission turned out to be valid, much to their chagrin. Fortunately, both survived the war and went on to build lives for themselves and their families. Scott was hospitalized on his return to the U.S. for several months to undergo treatment of his war wounds and injuries. He met the love of his life at this time and married her. He kept in touch with some of the 485th airmen through their reunion association and reunited with Seymour Segan at a 485th Bomb Group Association reunion in 1990. He had last seen Segan in Rumania, having visited him at a Rumanian hospital before he returned to Italy. Scott continued to experience pain from his injuries throughout the remainder of his life.

Many of the participants were decorated for bravery on that mission and some of the bravest actions were unknown or went unrecognized. For instance, several of the men on Crouchley's crew were recognized for wounds and for their actions on the mission. John Wilson and Eugene LaScotte both received medals, including the Purple Heart for wounds received and the Distinguished Flying Cross.

LaScotte returned to Minnesota, married and raised a family. Although he continued to have physical problems as a result of his bail out and imprisonment, he did not seek treatment through the Veterans Administration. He went blind in one eye, an apparent result of malnutrition while imprisoned in Bulgaria and this finally prompted him to seek treatment through the Veterans Administration in the 1980's. He lived a full life and died with his family close by in 2001.[1]

Figures 50 and 51-Sgt. Eugene LaScotte wearing Purple Heart and Distinguished Flying Cross medals on left and Lt. John Wilson on right receiving Purple Heart and Distinguished Flying Cross from Col. John Tomhave, commander of 485th Bomb Group.

So what happened to the crew of *Flak Shak*? We know what happened some of them. Volney Wiggins, the pilot, returned to his wife and civilian life in California at the end of the war. Tragically, he died in an auto accident in 1959.[2]

Ken Leasure, the navigator, returned to civilian life and went to law school. After starting his own law practice in Endicott, New York he went into politics and became a state assemblyman in New York, serving in that position from 1967-1972. He died in 2008.

The top turret gunner, Virgil Anderson, returned to Minnesota, married and raised his family there. He died in 2002.

Edward "Lyle" Hartupee, ball gunner on the Wiggins crew, died a suspicious death on February 17, 1949. He returned home with

Epilogue

some of the same demons that followed him in Italy and continued to drink heavily and experienced nightmares, according to relatives. He had apparently gone to a house or cabin that was used for hunting for "a rest". Several days later two friends found him on the road 1 ½ miles away, either walking or crawling. (The newspaper reports differed in their accounts.) According to one report Hartupee was ill and wouldn't say anything. His friends took him back to the house and made dinner for him. While preparing dinner the friends heard a shot in another room and went to the room to find Hartupee slumped on the floor with a wound in his stomach and a shotgun by his side. Hartupee died later that night at the hospital. His death was ruled a suicide and the coroner's finding was as troubling as the turns his life had taken The headline on one of the newspaper stories read "Funeral Monday for Air Force hero."[3]

Waist gunner Martin Caine remained in U.S. hospitals for more than a year after he returned. He attended law school, graduated and became a successful corporate attorney in New York City. He also met and married the love of his life, Lynn. They had one son and adopted a daughter. Caine had difficulty obtaining health insurance, due to his war injuries, and finally sought assistance with the Veterans Administration. He died of cancer in a V.A. hospital in 1971. His wife was grief-stricken and wanted to help other women in similar situations. She wrote a best-selling book entitled *Widow*, first released in 1974.[4]

Figure 52-Martin Caine (wearing sunglasses) playing cards in hospital in 1945

As for Bob Hickman, he wanted nothing further to do with the military upon his discharge in 1945. He worked in the construction business, marrying his wife Sarah, and raising her five children in Ohio. He had health issues over the years from injuries he suffered during the attacks on *Flak Shak,* particularly from the shrapnel wounds to his back. In 2005 he requested assistance through the Veterans Administration. Since he had never applied for benefits previously, there was no "paper trail" or record of previous treatment. What complicated matters was that the family home caught fire shortly after the war ended, destroying nearly everything, including all his military records and awards. Two of the airmen who were on this mission stepped forward and provided letters testifying to his injuries. One of the men was Ray Heskes, a buddy who visited him in the hospital in Bari. The other was Ken Leasure, who had bandaged his wounds which stopped the bleeding and likely saved his life that day. The V.A. benefits were granted. (See Appendices E and F.)[5]

Copilot William "Jack" Hays from Crouchley's crew, the last to be captured from that crew, believed his Boy Scout training aided him immensely in his evasion from the Bulgarian Army for several days. He believed these same skills helped him in his dark days as a prisoner in Shumen. He returned home, married, and raised a family. He dedicated his life to the Boy Scouts and served as a District Scout Executive in various places, including the Panama Canal Zone. He finished his career in the same capacity in Griffith, Georgia. He died in 2002 with his daughter, Harriet, by his side, caring for him.[6]

John Wilson, the navigator on Crouchley's crew, elected to stay in the Air Force after marrying. He went on to fly 25 combat missions in Korea with the 307th Bomb Wing. He later served in various capacities with the 55th Strategic Reconnaissance Wing, retiring after 23 years of service in 1963 with the rank of lieutenant colonel.[7]

Tail gunner William Van Meer died in 2005. He married, raised a family and stayed in the Air Force, serving in Korea and Vietnam.

Some of our European friends have taken steps to remember those who didn't survive. In faraway Poland, in the rural community of Zygodowice, local Poles have not forgotten the bomber that crashed in a farmer's field on September 13, 1944. Several of them helped bury Matt Hall and the other five men who died that day. Other locals came during the night, bringing flowers to the unmarked site, and praying for the souls of the men.[8]

Figure 53-Monument honoring Matt Hall and the crew of Captain William Lawrence in Zygodowice, Poland.

The Germans allowed no marker at the mass grave site. After the war ended, when Poland was under Russian control, the Americans returned and with the help of the locals, located the site and recovered the remains of the American flyers. Matt Hall didn't make it home for his 21st birthday. His remains were finally returned home to his family in Cuthbert, Georgia in May 1949 for burial.

But the Poles didn't forget. After they gained their freedom from Russia they built a monument to honor the men, but didn't have their names. In 1992, the Secretary of the Air Force, Donald Rice, heard of the matter and provided the crew names to the Poles. In 1994 a ceremony was held at the Polish Embassy in Washington D.C. to

Of Broad Stripes and Bright Stars

honor Matt Hall and his crew for their sacrifice. Four surviving crew members were presented the Polish War Cross. Matt's two sisters, Agnes and Elizabeth, accepted Matt's medal on his behalf. Flowers and candles still adorn the memorial site in Zygodowice year around, placed there by school children and each year a ceremony is held, honoring Matt and the others, on the anniversary of the crash date, September 13th.[9]

In Iepuresti, a few miles west of Bucharest, Rumania a high school teacher, Ovidiu Coca, learned of a nearby crash site of an American bomber, shot down during WWII. The plane had crashed on the Barbu farm. He met with one of the Barbu family, which resulted in a trip to the farm where he found pieces of an aircraft, including what was later determined to be a bomb bay door from a B-24. The door had been put to use as a cover for an outbuilding. His further research at a local church provided the names of some of the men on the crew, who were buried locally by the villagers. It was determined that these men were members of Lt. Sloan's crew.

Figure 54-Ovidiu Coca's classroom display

Coca took some of his students to the field where the bomber crashed and they searched and found more pieces of wreckage. Coca ultimately built a display at his school, his own "small museum" of sorts, for the benefit and education of his students, with bits of wreckage and the story of Sloan's crew. This is Coca's tribute to these men who lost their lives, so his students will learn the story about the crew who lost their lives on the nearby farm.[10]

The remains of all the men from the 485th Bomb Group who lost their lives on June 28, 1944 have been recovered, except for one, John "Dud" Crouchley. He remained at the controls of his crippled airplane, giving the crew time to bail out, in

Epilogue

essence giving them their lives at the cost of his own life. He was still flying the plane when it crashed in Bulgaria.

The American military mistakenly believed that Crouchley's plane had gone down near Bucharest, as reported in the Missing Air Crew Report and the Narrative Mission Statement of the 485th Bomb Group for June 28, 1944, the two surviving official records. The author, along with Dan Crouchley (Dud's nephew) and Stan Stanev, a retired Bulgarian army colonel and university professor, wanted to find the crash site, hoping to eventually bring Lt. Crouchley home. Stanev researched Bulgarian records and learned of a crash site of an American bomber from WWII near the village of Churen. Further research on his part revealed that a pilot by the name of "Krachali" was killed in the crash. Armed with this information he went to the region and located a crash site and found pieces of wreckage.

The author contacted DPMO (Defense POW/Missing Personnel Office) and provided investigator John Gray with this information. Dept. of Defense investigators went to the crash site with one of Stanev's colleagues in June 2007, recovering pieces of wreckage which were later positively identified as pieces of Crouchley's plane. A team of DPMO investigators, including Gray, returned in 2008 and Stanev accompanied them to the crash site. Another team from DPMO returned to gather information in 2010. At this time there has been no forensic excavation and Lt. Crouchley is still MIA (Missing in Action), the only one who has not returned from this mission.[11]

Figure 55-2nd Lt. John Crouchley

NOTES AND REFERENCES

[1] Obtained from several interviews with Mark LaScotte.

[2] This information came from Linda Haley, Bob Hickman's daughter, who learned this from Wiggins' widow.

[3] Missouri Death Certificate 9651 ruled the death a suicide from a gunshot wound, due to shock and loss of blood. Richard Bresnahan, Hartupee's nephew, researched the death, finding various newspaper accounts that provide more questions than answers. Bresnahan was told there were no additional surviving records (aside from the 2-page death certificate). It's unknown whether or not there was an actual law enforcement investigation into the death. Shotgun suicides in the stomach are not a common occurrence and the Hartupee family was always suspicious of the coroner's finding. The box on the death certificate was left unchecked regarding whether or not an autopsy was performed.

[4] Obtained from 7/5/14 phone interview with Jonathan Caine, Martin's son.

[5] Bob Hickman is still alive and living in Ohio.

[6] Obtained from 8/1/14 email letter written by Harriet Butchko Hays.

[7] Obtained from 7/7/14 email letter by John Wilson Jr.

[8] The airmen were buried in a mass, unmarked grave and the local residents were ordered to stay away from the site and threatened with incarceration at Oswiecim (Auschwitz) if they were found there.

[9] The author attended the 60th anniversary ceremony in 2004. He spoke at the gathering, representing the families of the airmen, and presented a WWII airman's dress uniform to Zygmunt Kraus, curator of a local private museum built to honor the crew.

[10] Coca worked with the author to identify the crew and continues to search for new details on the crash.

[11] Much of the background on the search for Lt. Crouchley is from the author's personal research and involvement in this matter. In addition to the information included in the story, the author also met with Dept. of Defense investigator John Gray and other DPMO researchers to discuss this case in Washington D.C. in 2009.

Appendix A

Bob Hickman V.A. Summary

SERVICE NUMBER:	~~[redacted]~~	
CATEGORY:	CODE:	EXPLANATION:
RANK:	2	Enlisted Man
ARM OF SERVICE:	12	Air Force, Transport/Bombardment Units
AGE:	19	19
RACE:	1	White, includes Mexican
YEARS OF SVC:	16	1 Year(s), 6 Month(s)
MO/YR OF ADMISION:	064	June 1944
STATION OF ADMISSION:	-3	European Area
DAY OF ADMISSION	28	28
FINAL TRMT FACILITY:	7	General hospital
INVALID/DIED IN PRSN:	0	Not a special classification
TYPE OF CASE:	4	Casualty, battle
TYPE OF ADMISSION:	1	New
TYPE OF DIAGNOSIS:	1	Sole diagnosis, no history of prior disease, injury or battle casualty
LINE OF DUTY:	1	In line of duty
FIRST DIAGNOSIS:	0265	Fracture, compound, depressed, of skull with no nerve or artery involvement
LOCATION:	0302	Cranium, Face and Neck (excl. vertebral): Parietal bone
OPERATION:	184	Elevation of depressed fragments for skull fracture
SECOND DIAGNOSIS:	-	Not Found
LOCATION:	-	Not Found
OPERATION:	-	Not Found
THIRD DIAGNOSIS:	-	Not Found
CAUSATIVE AGENT:	034	Shell Fragment, Flak, Shrapnel
FINAL RESULT:	-	Not Found
DISPOSITION:	6	Duty
FIELD OF CAUSE OF		

Appendix B

(Silver Star citation for *Flak Shak* crew)

SECTION II - AWARDS OF THE SILVER STAR

　　　　＊　　　　　　　　　＊　　　　　　　　　＊

3. For gallantry in action as crew of a B-24 type aircraft. On 28 June 1944, this crew participated in a bombing mission against highly important and vital enemy oil fields in Rumania. Enroute to the target severe enemy opposition in the form of intense and accurate anti-aircraft fire and enemy fighters was encountered, inflicting grave damage to the aircraft this gallant crew was flying, and seriously wounding the bombardier. Despite the damaged condition of their aircraft and continued heavy enemy opposition, these men skillfully maintained their lead position, thereby completing a highly successful bombing run. the bombardier displayed great courage in releasing his bombs despite his severe wound. Rallying from the target their aircraft was savagely attacked by eight enemy fighters, who singled out their crippled aircraft and made seven aggressive attacks before being finally driven away. Despite the seriousness and almost uncontrollable condition of their aircraft these courageous crewmen remained at their stations and succeeded in warding off the enemy aircraft. Nine of these crew members were seriously wounded by the enemy fighter fire, but in the face of disaster destroyed six of the hostile aircraft. The pilot, co-pilot and navigator displayed great technique in pulling the aircraft out of a steep dive and bringing it safely back to an advanced allied air field without the protection of other friendly aircraft. By their gallant action, firm determination to successfully complete their mission, and their sincere devotion to duty this gallant crew has upheld the highest traditions of the Military Service, thereby reflecting great credit upon themselves and the Armed Forces of the United States of America.

Appendix C

TO WHOM IT MAY CONCERN:

February 1, 2005

I, KENNETH S LEASURE, have prepared and signed this statement of fact at the request of ROBERT HICKMAN, 258 Baron Ct., Reynoldsburg, Ohio, 43068.

On June 28, 1944, I was the Navigator on a B-24 Liberator Bomber based in Venosa, Italy with the 15th Air Force, 485th Bomb Group, 831st Squadron on a mission to Ploesti Oil Fields and Bucharest, Romania. My rank was First Lt. and my Serial Number was 0-759813.

During the bomb run we encountered very heavy anti-aircraft fire and lost our outboard, right-wing engine over the target. After our bombs were dropped, the aircraft fell sharply out of formation and down to the right. We were immediately attacked by several ME 109 fighter aircraft of the German Air Force.. A running battle then ensued.. We lost a second engine on the left wing. We could not hold altitude with the remainder of our squadron and were soon alone with the attackers at 10,000 feet. Our gunners, including Sgt. Hickman, were later credited with 6-7 "kills" by the time the fighters broke contact.

Every member of the ten-man crew (except the radio operator) suffered injuries from flack 50 caliber machine gun fire and 20 mm cannon fire.. Injuries ranged from moderate to near fatal. There was no possibility of "bailing out" with so many injured crewmen on board.

We (Capt. Wiggins and I) decided to try to get to the Yugoslav coast and ditch the plane along the shoreline. We had no hydraulics and no radio. Those of us who could then began to go through the aircraft applying tourniquets, morphine, bandages and shredding parachutes for bandage material to our injured crewmen.

It was at this time that I found Sgt. Hickman (the tail gunner) unconscious and still in his gun turret. I got him out and into the waist of the aircraft, gave him first-aid, stopped the bleeding and bandaged his wounds.

We reached the coast of Italy without further incident and crash-landed on an emergency air strip nearby. When I last saw Sgt. Hickman that day he was conscious and stable.

Though the Flak Shack never flew again, subsequently every member of the crew was awarded the Silver Star as a result of their heroic actions on that day.

Kenneth S. Leasure

Photo and Illustration Credits

Figure 1   Eugene LaScotte family
Figure 2   485th Bomb Group
Figure 3   485th Bomb Group
Figure 4   Virgil Anderson family
Figure 5   Robert Hickman family
Figure 6   Virgil Anderson family
Figure 7   485th Bomb Group
Figure 8   Allen Meister
Figure 9   Perry Monroe family
Figure 10   Bjorn Larson
Figure 11   Bjorn Larson
Figure 12   Bjorn Larson
Figure 13   Bjorn Larson
Figure 14   485th Bomb Group
Figure 15   Bill Harrington
Figure 16   Perry Monroe family
Figure 17   Perry Monroe family
Figure 18   Perry Monroe family
Figure 19   Perry Monroe family
Figure 20   Perry Monroe family
Figure 21   Perry Monroe family
Figure 22   Agnes Hall
Figure 23   485th Bomb Group
Figure 24   Virgil Anderson family
Figure 25   Bob Hickman
Figure 26   Virgil Anderson family
Figure 27   Wilson Shimer
Figure 28   Virgil Anderson family
Figure 29   Virgil Anderson family
Figure 30   Wilson Shimer
Figure 31   Wilson Shimer
Figure 32   Wilson Shimer
Figure 33   Wilson Shimer
Figure 34   Virgil Anderson family
Figure 35   Wilson Shimer
Figure 36   485th Bomb Group photo
Figure 37   485th Bomb Group photo
Figure 38   485th Bomb Group photo
Figure 39   Eugene LaScotte family
Figure 40   J.F. Wilson Jr. collection
Figure 41   J.F. Wilson Jr. collection
Figure 42   J.F. Wilson Jr. collection
Figure 43   J.F. Wilson Jr. collection
Figure 44   J.F. Wilson Jr. collection
Figure 45   Dan Crouchley
Figure 46   485th Bomb Group
Figure 47   Harriet Hays Butchko
Figure 48   J.F. Wilson Jr. collection
Figure 49   Roger Nichols family
Figure 50   Eugene LaScotte family
Figure 51   J.F. Wilson Jr. collection
Figure 52   Jonathan Caine
Figure 53   Elliott S. Dushkin
Figure 54   Ovidiu Coca
Figure 55   Dan Crouchley

Bibliography

485th Bomb Group Association. *Missions by the Numbers: Combat Missions Flown by the 485th Bomb Group*. Walnut Creek, California: Tarnaby, 2008.

Eamon, Gail and Jim. *By God We Made It: The War experiences of Vernon Christensen 1942-1945*. Colorado Springs, Colorado: Eamon family, 2002.

Johnson, Robert. *gidi gidi boom boom: The True Story of the Plane and Crew in WWII Europe*. San Ramon, California: Tarnaby, 2006.

Muirhead, John. *Those Who Fall: An Unforgettable Chronicle of War in the Air*. New York: Random House, 1986.

Palmer, Charles. *The Shumen Diary (A Personal Memoir)*. Morro Bay, California: Private printing, revised edition, 2004.

Schneider, Sammy. *This Is How It Was*. St. Petersburg, Florida: Southern Heritage Press, 1995.

Stanev, Stanimir and LaScotte, Mark. 289 Days Near Shumen: *An Album of the WWII Shumen POW Camp*. Shumen, Bulgaria: Konstantin Prevlasky University Press, 2012.

Whiting, Jerry. *Don't Let the Blue Star Turn Gold*: Downed Airmen in Europe in WWII. Walnut Creek, California: Tarnaby, 2005.

Wiktor, Stefan and Kowalczyk, Tadeusz. Wartime Memoirs from Zygodowice and its surroundings 1939-1945. (English translation of Polish title.) Private printing, 1992

Unpublished Private Documents

Albrecht, Mary T., story of Crouchley crew entitled "B-24, Miss Yankee Rebel", written in the Fall of 2001.

Dahlberg, Henry, 831st Bomb Sqdn engineering officer. Personal diary entries June 29, July 1 and July 2, 1944.

Douglas, John, 485th Bomb Group public relations officer. September 1944 press release regarding Wiggins crew.

Fiedler, Art, 325th Fighter Group pilot. Personal email letter to Mark LaScotte re: June 28, 1944 mission, January 22, 2011.

Grubb, Paul, 830th Bomb Sqdn tail gunner, Personal letter to 485th Historian from original crew member on *Nudist Kay* regarding loss of aircraft on 6/28/44.

Hall, Matthew, 831st Bomb Sqdn copilot. Personal letters home November 1, 1943-September 12, 1944.

Harrington, William, 831st Bomb Sqdn bombardier. Personal diary entries, June 28 and July 2, 1944.

Heskes, Ray, 831st Bomb Sqdn ball gunner. Personal email letter to Jerry Whiting re: his observations on the June 28, 1944 mission and diary entry, October 6, 2007. In addition, a February 1, 2005 personal letter to V.A. attesting to tail gunner Bob Hickman's injuries.

Hickman, Robert, 831st Bomb Sqdn tail gunner. Hospital Admission Card with injury summary, Office of the Surgeon General, Dept. of the Army, for 1944.

Johnson, E.G., 828th Bomb Sqdn ball gunner. Personal letter to John Wilson, September 28, 1988.

LaScotte, Eugene, 828th Bomb Sqdn nose gunner. Two personal letters home from Shumen POW camp, July 1944. Personal letters to John Wilson, September 1 and September 22, 1988, November 2, 1988 and

January 11, 1989. Personal letter to Veterans Administration, dated October 28, 1982.

Leasure, Kenneth, 485th Bomb Group, navigator on *Flak Shak*-February 1, 2005 letter to the V.A. a personal witness statement attesting to tail gunner Bob Hickman's injuries.

Leveille, Forrest, 828th Bomb Sqdn bombardier. Personal letter to Dianne LaScotte, dated March 3, 2005, regarding the Crouchley crew.

Mattison, Richard F., 828th Bomb Sqdn nose gunner. Personal diary entry for June 28, 1944.

Monroe, Perry, 828th Bomb Sqdn ball gunner. Personal diary/flight log, May 5, 1944-September 5, 1944.

Monroe, Roger, 828th Bomb Sqdn pilot, operations officer. Personal diary.

Nichols, Roger, 828th Bomb Sqdn pilot. Personal letters home, July 29, 1944 and August 6, 1944 regarding the June 28, 1944 mission.

Scott, James, 829th Bomb Sqdn waist gunner. Personal typed account of June 28, 1944 mission to Bucharest, Rumania.

Wiggins, Volney, 831st Bomb Sqdn pilot. Personal letter to Jean Hall, September 13, 1944 regarding Matt Hall's MIA status.

Interviews

Anderson, Virgil, 485th Bomb Group, top turret gunner on *Flak Shak*-July 1998 personal interview by Ron and Vicky Rabe regarding the crew of *Flak Shak* and the June 28, 1944 mission.

Blodgett, Dan, 485th Bomb Group navigator-January 25, 2004 telephone interview by Jerry Whiting regarding Matt Hall's death.

Bobier, Bob, 485th Bomb Group pilot, former Shumen, Bulgaria POW-February 26, 2004 telephone interview by Jerry Whiting regarding the Shumen, Bulgaria POW camp.

Caine, Jonathan, son of Martin Caine-July 5, 2014 telephone interview by Jerry Whiting regarding his father's injuries suffered on June 28, 1944 mission and other details about his life.

Canin, Paul, 485th Bomb Group radar navigator-January 14, 2004 interview by Jerry Whiting in Walnut Creek, California, regarding Matt Hall's death.

Christensen, Vernon, 485th Bomb Group top turret gunner-January 14, 2004 and January 20, 2004 interviews by Jerry Whiting in Walnut Creek, California regarding Matt Hall's death.

Doyle, Richard 485th Bomb Group bombardier, former Shumen, Bulgaria POW-February 7, 2005 telephone interview by Jerry Whiting regarding the Shumen, Bulgaria POW camp.

Hickman, Robert, 485th Bomb Group, tail gunner on *Flak Shak*-January 19, 2011 and June 20, 2014 telephone interviews by Jerry Whiting regarding the crew of *Flak Shak* and the June 28, 1944 mission.

LaScotte, Eugene, 485th Bomb Group nose gunner-July 28, 1998 personal audio-taped interview by Dianne LaScotte regarding the June 28, 1944 mission.

Martin, Al, 485th Bomb Group waist gunner-March 29, 2011 telephone interview by Jerry Whiting regarding his observations on the June 28, 1944 mission.

Shimer, Wilson, 485th Bomb Group, flight engineer/waist gunner on *Flak Shak*-March 22, 2011 telephone interview by Jerry Whiting regarding the crew of *Flak Shak* and the June 28, 1944 mission.

Skryzynska, Maria, Polish witness-September 14, 2004 interview by Jerry Whiting in Zygodowice, Poland regarding the burial site of the William Lawrence crew (including Matt Hall) and local farmers efforts to maintain the site and memorialize the crew.

Stumpf, Roland, 98th Bomb Group pilot, former Shumen, Bulgaria POW-February 25, 2005 telephone interview by Jerry Whiting regarding the Shumen, Bulgaria POW camp.

Wiktor, Stefan, Polish witness-September 14, 2004 interview by Jerry Whiting in Zygodowice, Poland regarding the burial of Matt Hall.

Williams, Bill, 485th Bomb Group ball gunner-July 6, 2014 and July 13, 2014 telephone interviews by Jerry Whiting regarding ball turret and radio communication procedures.

U.S. Government Archival Information

USAF Historical Research Center, Maxwell Alabama. 15th Air Force Mission Reports, June 28, 1944, Reel A6464.

USAF Historical Research Center, Maxwell Alabama. 485th Bomb Group Unit History, Reel 0643.

USAF Historical Research Center, Maxwell Alabama. The Hall Mission to Bulgaria, Reel 6088.

NARA, College Park, Maryland. Missing Air Crew Reports (MACRs) of the U.S. Army Air Forces, 1941-1948.

Index

A
Aborjaily, Alfred 20,34,36
Adriatic Sea 12,23,25, 34,35,43,46
Algiers 21
Altamura, Italy 23
Anderson, Virgil 14,16,17, 39,40,44,45,47,5154,58,85, 88,101,105
Auschwitz, Poland 2,53,94

B
Baldridge, Colonel 79
Barber, Ben 43,46,47
Barbu family 92
Bari 12,24,36,37,46,84,90
Benson, Minnesota 16
Boise, Idaho 13,16
Boney, Maurice 18
Bresnahan, Richard 94
Brittain, Francis 14,16,40, 45,51-53
Buchanauer, Peter 58,85
Bucharest, Rumania 2,3,6,9, 11,12,25-28,58,61,81-83,92,93,105
Burrows, Webster 58
Butchko, Harriet 94,101

C
Caine, Martin 14,16,17,42-45,47,50-54,89,94,101,106
Canin, Paul 55,106
Chitila Marshalling Yard 12,83
Churen, Bulgaria 93

Coca, Ovidiu 92
Cochinesti, Rumania 31
Crouchley, John 8,65,85,66,93

D
Danube River 25,67
Dempsey, John 14,15,39-41,45,47,51-53
Durden, Jerry 20,33,34,38

F
Fairmont, Nebraska 13,16
Flak Shak 2,8,13,39,40, 41,43,47,51,88,90,97,105,106
Florisdorf Oil Refinery 7
Friedrichschafen, Germany 38

G
Georgia 14,16,90,91
Geneva Convention 76
gidi gidi boom boom 79
Gray, John 94
Griffith, Georgia 90

H
Halcomb, Fales 20,33,34,88
Haley, Linda 21,94
Hall, Matt 2,13,14,39, 53,54,55,91,92,105,106,107
Hall, William 79
Hanson, John 29
Harrington, Bill 29,31,101

Hartupee, Edward 13,14,16,17,41,44,45,51-53,88,89,94,
Hayes, Stacy 14
Hays, William 66,67, 74,76,85,90,101,94
Heskes, Ray 21,90,104
Hickman Bob 2,15,89, 94,95,101,104,105
Hirsch, Milton 58,63,84
Hogan, Captain 29
Hollowell, Bill 18,70, 73,76,78,79,85
Hufstader, Rodney. 29

I
Iepuresti, Rumania 92

J
Johnson, Captain James 51
Johnson, Ed 66-73,78,85,104
Johnson, Robert 79
Jordan, Dick 6,17,58,84

K
Karlova, Bulgaria 12,25,82
Kraus, Zygmunt 94

L
Langstaff, Thomas 66, 67,72,73,85
LaScotte Eugene 5,7,18, 21,23,24,30,66,67,69-75,78,87,88,94,101,103, 104,105,106
Leasure, Ken 14,15, 40,41,44,45,51-53,88,90,105
Leveille, Forrest 18,105,21,66

M
Mack, George 19,20,34,74
Martin, Al 59,64,106
Maurer, Herman 19,20,34
Meister, Allen 18,66,101
Miss Yankee Rebel 18,19,104
Monroe, Perry 20,21, 33,34,37,38,101,
Monroe, Ralph 11
Munich 9
My Brother and I 19,33,37

N
Narrative Mission Report 2, 30,31,85,
New Mexico 15
New York 16,88,89,103
North Africa 12
Nudist Kay 17,57,58,104

O
O'Connor, Horace 18,58,85
Ohio 15,90,94
Oswiecim, Poland 2,53,94
Owen, Hudson 8,19,20,33-36

P
Pantanella, Italy 11
Pennsylvania 15,16
Perillo, Ralph 66,67, 72,73,78,85
Peterson, Clayton 58,84
Peterson, Scott 59,61
Ploesti, Rumania 6,9,12
Ponte, Ken 20,33,34,35,38+
Prahova Oil Refinery 11,12

R

Roberts, Bill 33,34
Rumania 11,12,26,52,60-64,83,85,87,92,105

S

Salt Lake City, Utah 14
Sardinia 19
Scott, James 6,7,17,18,21,24,30,57-64,85,87
Segan, Seymour 58,60,61,84,87
Shimer, Wilson 1,14,16,17,44,101
Shumen, Bulgaria POW camp 76-79,90,103-106
Silver Star medal 2,52,53,54,97
Sloan, Robert 17,29,30,31,84,92
Smith, Robert 11,27
Smith, Walter 77,79
Spinazzola, Italy 11,23
S.S. Paul Hamilton 10,21
St. Paul, Minnesota 5
Stanev, Stan 93

T

Titan Oil Refinery 11,12,27,29
Turner, Donald 66,68,69,71,73,74,78,85

Tyer, Ivan 6,8,17,57,58,84
Tyer's Flyers 17

V

Van Meer, William 66,67,68,71,73,78,85,90
Venosa, Italy 12,15,30,47,51,52,82
Vienna, Austria 5,7,9,10,19
Villagio Mancuso 21

W

Wiener Neustadt, Austria 9
Wiggins, Volney 13-16,39,40,41,43,45,46,51,52,53,88,94,104,105
Wiktor, Stefan 55
Wilson, John 18,21,69,78,79,85,87,88,90,94,104,

Y

Yaeger, Major 64
Yugoslavia 41,43,46,71,74

Z

Zygodowice, Poland 55,91,92,103,106,107

The Author

Jerry Whiting was born in Sioux Falls, South Dakota where he spent his early years and moved to the San Francisco Bay Area when he was in high school. He obtained a bachelor's degree from the University of California, Santa Barbara and a master's degree from John F. Kennedy University.

He worked as a probation counselor before becoming a police officer in California. During his 25-year career he worked in a variety of assignments in the Patrol and Detective divisions and was also a hostage negotiator. On one special project he worked with several police departments in Europe and on another he worked with the tribal police on the Cheyenne River Sioux Indian Reservation.

Jerry with U.S. Navy Commander Renee Richardson from DPMO (2010 photo)

Ultimately Jerry took an early retirement to pursue a writing career. An avid student of history, he and his father collaborated on his first book, *I'm Off To War, Mother, But I'll Be Back*. This book chronicled his dad's experience as a B-24 tail gunner in WWII. Other WWII books followed, including *Don't Let the Blue Star Turn Gold* and *Veterans in the Mist*. He also published the group history for the 485th Bomb Group, *Missions by the Numbers*.

In addition to writing Jerry interviewed Vets for other projects, including documentaries. In this regard he ventured out on his own, producing two WWII documentaries, *In the Shadow of Mt. Vulture* and *New Year's at Ramitelli: A Safe Haven for Change*. He has consulted with DPMO on MIA cases and provided a training seminar to that agency a few years ago, in hopes of facilitating the recovery of some of our missing airmen.

Jerry has been the featured speaker at various events across the U.S. and abroad. He has given presentations in Italy, Poland and Germany in his areas of expertise regarding WWII. He and his wife, Ann, live in Walnut Creek, California with their golden retriever, Barney. You can learn more about his works on his website at www.jwhitingwarstories.com and contact Jerry directly by email at EAJWWhiting@aol.com with any questions or requests.

www.ingramcontent.com/pod-product-compliance
Lightning Source LLC
Chambersburg PA
CBHW061447040426
42450CB00007B/1262